Embarking On The Way
A Guide to Western Taoism

Solala Towler

Abode of the Etenal Tao
Eugene, Oregon

The Abode of the Eternal Tao
1991 Garfield St.
Eugene, OR 97405

Web site: http://www.abodetao.com/

Quotations from the *Tao Te Ching* by Lao Tsu, translated by Feng/ English Copyright 1972 by Gia-fu Feng and Jane English. Reprinted by permission of Alfred A. Knopf Inc.

Cover art from White Clouds Temple in Beijing.

Printed in the United States of America.

ISBN 0-9649912-2-5

*Dedicated to all students of the Way,
past, present and future.*

Acknowledgments

I wish to honor and give thanks to my teachers, both in this lifetime and in countless past ones. It is to them that I owe what little progress I have made upon the Way.

In that spirit I thank David Cheng, Hua-Ching Ni, Chen Hui Xian, Chungliang Al Huang and Chen Fu Yin.

I would also like to thank my tireless and open minded editor, Cher Mikkola, for her patience and warm hearted assistance with this book.

And lastly, my wife and life partner, Christine, for her priceless love and support, without which I would not have had the patience, fortitude and audacity to write a book about Taoism.

Foreword

So often, I am asked to explain about Chinese spirituality, about the "religion" in China. Usually, following a necessary, longwinded exploration of its many facets, I conclude by saying, "The Chinese adopt, adapt and assimilate all great spiritual traditions, and put them into a melting pot called TAO, to be continually distilled by ever-changing and transforming alchemy into a present-day elixir for sensible and pragmatic living."

It has been the same process in my own life. Born and raised in a traditional Chinese family through adolescence, steeped in the teachings of Taoism, Confucianism, Buddhism, and later, mixed with Christian missionary and other religious infiltrations, I have learned to disseminate and absorb the most useful ingredients to serve my own needs, endeavoring to follow the Way to become a more balanced and integrated human being.

Uprooted from Chinese soil since my late teens, I have lived more than four decades in America and traveled most parts of the world. I call myself a Taoist by heart and in practice. But it is clear that the "Tao that can be Taoed" by other Taoists is not necessarily the Tao I am living by. Likewise, the tai ji I practice is often different from the tai ji many others follow. My Tao teaching and learning that have inspired me, from day to day, are variations apart from the ways of traditionalists and discriminating academicians.

Nevertheless, I have found my destiny and have followed my own way to be a perpetual student and grateful teacher of this eternal, yet constantly revelatory Tao. In the past twenty-five years, through my worldwide network of the Living Tao Foundation, I have shared this evolving lifelong learning with thousands of kindred souls.

It is a pleasure for me to recommend this "uncarved and un-bleached" assemblage of reflections by a contemporary Taoist, Solala Towler. As a Westerner, he has found his own unique way to make many essential connections to the Tao, and is able to bring together his inquiries into an easily digestible and congenial banquet. He invites novices and long-time journeyers to pause along their way to taste a few enticing morsels with him.

Throughout my network I have supported and have expressed gratitude for Solala's journal of contemporary Taoism, *The Empty Vessel* and I have applauded his many accomplishments in bringing a diverse group of practitioners of Tao to share modern Taoism in everyday living. I am especially delighted to find this current contribution surprisingly enlightening. It is easy to suspend my critical reservations regarding historic authenticity or anecdotal accuracyies. I trust his genuine wish to re-create what he has assimilated in his own learning as a Westerner. It is refreshing, and often eye-opening to revisit some of these old stories as new again.

In traditional Chinese fashion I welcome Solala Towler's offering with this classic rejoinder; about the complementarity of West and East:

A Chinese Taoist meets two Western friends for an alfresco dinner. On their first toasting of wine, the Westerners joyfully declare, "Cheers to the three of us!" The Chinese hastens to add, "To the seven of us! Let's include the bright full moon and these three silhouettes of such good friends dancing on the ground."

Cheers! Join us, readers, to sample a few humble plates of Taoist offerings and, "Gun Bei" (Bottoms up)! Enjoy living your own, very special Tao!

Chungliang Al Huang
Living Tao Foundation

Chungliang Al Huang is the founder-president of the International Living Tao Foundation and the director of Lan Ting Institute. He is the author of the seminal classic *Embrace Tiger, Return to Mountain: The Essence of Tai Ji, Quantum Soup,* and co-author with Alan Watts of *Tao: The Watercourse Way,* and with Jerry Lynch of *Thinking Body, Dancing Mind; Mentoring: The Tao of Giving and Receiving Wisdom;* and *Working Out, Working Within: The Tao of Inner Fitness Through Sports and Exercise.*

Preface

One of the most beloved books in China is *The Journey to the West* first published in 1592. It tells the story of the sixteen year pilgrimage of a monk named Hsuan-tsang (596-664) and his journey to India in quest of Buddhist scriptures. Along the way he is helped by four animal disciples, including the outrageous Monkey. This is a fascinating story, filled with Buddhist and Taoist alchemical and religious imagery.

Lao Tzu, the author of the "Taoist bible," the *Tao Te Ching*, is said to have gone off into the Western wilderness after leaving an increasingly fractured society, never to be heard from again. Later on, a collection of his oral teachings was compiled under the title *Hua Hu Ching*. At one point in China's history, when Buddhism and Taoism were in conflict, a certain Taoist sect spread the story that the Buddha was actually Lao Tzu who had traveled to India!

The move to the West continues today. In my previous book, *A Gathering of Cranes: Bringing the Tao to the West*, I interviewed nine teachers, all of whom had come from China to the West to teach, to live, to learn. It was fascinating to hear how living in the West had enhanced and sometimes altered their way of teaching and practicing. As well, it was interesting to hear how they thought Taoist practices and philosophy would affect the West.

This time I have produced a work to introduce Western students to the ways of the East. Taoism may have originated in China but it is truly a universal path, one which anyone can follow, be they from the East or the West.

Some teachers say that Western followers of the Tao will have an impact on Taoism in China one day. One contemporary Taoist master, Hua-Ching Ni says, "Only after the ancient arts are accepted by wise Westerners will the Chinese come back to what was devalued and neglected." This book is an attempt to educate Western readers and de-mystify some of the ancient wisdom of the Tao.

On another note: the transliteration of Chinese is always awkward. There are so many ways of spelling each word—such as qi, chi, chee, etc. While in my text I have mostly used the modern pinyin version (except for the word Tao itself, since so many Westerners are already familiar with that spelling), many of the sources quoted in the book use a variety of ways of spelling. Thus the reader may sometimes become confused by the plethora of spellings of qigong, chee gong, chi kung and so on. I apologize for that and hope the reader will be able to follow along with a spirit of openness and patience.

Contents

Introduction

Why Western Taoism?

Today we live in a world rife with problems of every kind: environmental, political, economic, religious and interpersonal. Everywhere we look we see pain, suffering, degradation. Many people feel cut off, alone, unneeded and inconsequential. Hypocritical religious demagogues preach to the converted, the poor, the lonely. The homeless are everywhere, even in the once proud United States, staring out at us with sad and desperate eyes. The delicate ecological balance of our planet seems hopelessly upset; the threat of nuclear annihilation only serves to distract us from fears of new plagues or the ever growing ranks of chronic ills that seem to elude our finest medical minds.

Meanwhile, divorce rates and child abuse statistics continue to soar. We are increasingly aware of just how dysfunctional the family life of the last few generations really has been. The solace that traditional religions once offered seems to be losing more ground each day.

What can Taoism, a six thousand year old philosophy of ancient China, have to offer at this crucial time? We may begin by asking just what Taoism is—or in asking what it is we might begin by saying what it is not. It is not a new religion. It is not a New Age movement, though aspects of it have been taken up by many so called New Age practitioners. It is not a cult or movement led by overbearing personalities.

Taoism is a *living philosophy*. While its traditions and practices go back thousands of years, it is also born anew each moment. The Tao itself, being beyond explanations, rationalizations, or descriptions, moves on its magnificent way, carrying all of us with it whether we are conscious of it or not, whether we even care or not. But oh what a ride it can be if we allow ourselves to awaken to the thrill of it, the glory of it, the deep down everyday simple pleasure of it!

Taoism offers us a simple, down to earth, practical way of being and living, a way of comporting ourselves on our journey between birth and death and beyond.

In Taoism we can find a way of being, a way of accepting, a way of working *with* rather than *against* the changes that life may bring us. Wonderfully illustrative texts such as the *Tao Te Ching* and *Chuang Tzu* offer inspiration, illumination, and expedient advice on life, death and all that lies between. In Chinese medicine we can find cure and comfort for many modern and not-so-modern ills and complaints for which our present day technological medicine has nothing to offer. With Taoist health practices such as qigong (chee gong) and tai ji quan we can find ways to stabilize and balance our bodies, allowing us to lead long-lasting and healthy lives. Taoist sexual yoga can guide us gracefully through the tricky and often dangerous labyrinth of human sexuality.

And lastly, through Taoist meditation practices we may finally arrive at that precious point of power described in Taoist tradition as Returning to the Source—the source of our own being as well as being-ness itself.

Today's problems are real, concrete and seemingly unresolvable. They call for something besides fantasies and visions, something that can be applied to everyday life with its everyday problems. Taoism offers not a way out but a way *through*. Its solutions are real, concrete and eminently applicable, regardless of one's race, religion or gender. Although Taoists have been called dreamy eyed mystics, nothing could be further from the truth. What the ancient masters learned through countless years of observation and practice can be just as useful today as it was in the time of the Yellow Emperor, perhaps more so.

Many Westerners, impressed by the culture and history of the East, are drawn to its thought, art, music, food, medicine and philosophies. But Taoism is not just an ancient, foreign, mystical path. In truth, it is trans-cultural, non-sexist, practical yet scientific. Its practices work on many levels—physical, emotional, psychological and spiritual. It is extremely ancient yet completely up to date. It can be applied to political action, environmental concerns, economic interests, emotional clearing, health problems, business enterprises, psychological balance, sexuality and spiritual fulfillment. It works well for highly individuated Westerners and can be approached on any level, from the rank beginner to the evolved aspirant. There is nothing to join, no vows to take, no special naming, clothing style or diet to follow. It is strictly up to the individual to apply whatever aspect of the tradition he or she wishes. The emphasis is on self cultivation: we tend our own spiritual garden— we water it with our tears of joy and sadness, fertilize it with the "bullshit" of our lives, weed out the negative influences with our own hard work and then reap and enjoy the harvest.

This book is not a scholarly tour of Chinese Taoism. I am not a scholar, not a master or *sifu*, not an enlightened being speaking from on high. I am a life-long seeker of truth and spiritual fulfillment and have applied Taoist teachings and practices to my own often challenging life. The proof of their efficacy is in my own healing, my own spiritual evolution (such as it is) and a greater understanding of my place within the vast and often chaotic universe we call Tao.

This is, foremost, a guide to Western Taoism. I have tried to hold to the teachings of the ancient achieved ones such as Lao Tzu and Chuang Tzu who are models of introspection, enlightenment and engagement with the world. I have also looked toward modern teachers and masters I have studied with, either through their books or personally. Of course, any wisdom found in these pages is inspired by my teachers, both living and dead, and any mistakes, personal opinions or theories are entirely my own.

I am offering you a smorgasbord of Taoist delights. You may come to the table and eat to your heart's content, by either picking and choosing just what dishes speak to your own heart and stomach or by partaking of the whole feast. There is no need to renounce your own religion or spiritual path to savor this delightful meal. The practices of meditation, qigong, tai ji or Chinese medicine are not limited to Taoists only. They are for everyone, regardless of religion, creed, nationality, race, gender, age or political persuasion.

Many people, when they hear Taoist teachings, say "Why, that's just how I feel! I must be a Taoist and didn't know it!" These people have often felt like oddballs all their lives, having never found a particular religion or belief system that spoke directly to them. Much like Native American spirituality, Taoism is an earth-based path. It venerates nature as the highest teacher. Indeed, many of the movements of qigong and tai ji are taken directly from the natural world of birds and other animals. In Taoism, the emphasis is not on getting up and out of the body and the material plane, but to plumb ever deeper the dark, mysterious and watery depths of Mother Earth, the Yin, the Mysterious Female Principle.

Taoism looks at the physical plane as a very real and very useful place, one where we can use the intrinsic and powerful energy of our bodies—our qi—in order to enhance and further ourselves as spiritual beings. It does not shy away from using all our interests, mental as well as physical, in that quest for perfect wholeness and oneness with the divine or Tao.

High in the mountains of China at the ancient Taiqing Temple on Lao Shan my friends and I met with the temple abbot. As we drank cup after cup of the flavorsome green tea that is grown on the mountain, we listened as Abbot Liu told us that "Taoism is all based on the study of nature. Study the ways of nature and you can't go wrong."

"We have common points, you and I," he continued. "American people love nature. American people love peace. They pursue good health. They have many common points with Taoism, so it is very natural for them to study Taoism. American people also have a lot of scientific achievement. I think that if they can combine Taoist ideas and scientific achievement they will be very strong. Study Taoism bit by bit, one thing or aspect at a time. I know that American people love freedom, freedom of the individual. Develop Taoism in America according to the reality of America."

Abbot Liu's words ring true. If Taoism is to be effective in the West, then it should be developed according to the reality of the West. There are aspects of traditional Chinese Taoism that I think will never really catch on in our culture. They include the use of talismans, chanting of sutra-like books, exorcisms, bowing to numerous statues of various divinities and extreme and even dangerous meditation and qigong practices. Religious Taoism, as it is practiced today in China, is a blend of the philosophical Taoism of Lao Tzu and Chuang Tzu, magical folk religion, Buddhism and even Confucianism. The volumes of the Taoist canon run into the thousands. Temples are filled with statues of benign and wrathful deities, Buddhist saints, and even historical figures such as military generals. Taoism is divided into many sects, all with their own traditions and practices. Some adherents are celibate, some are vegetarians, some are neither. Practices vary widely and various lineages claim direct descent from Lao Tzu himself, who today is venerated as a god-like being and worshipped along with the Jade Emperor who rules over a hierarchical Taoist heaven. Many temples are in reality only fronts to attract tourists dollars and have nothing to do with the ancient centers of worship and study.

None of this need concern us in the West. I believe that if we stick to the basic teachings and traditions of Lao Tzu, Chuang Tzu, Lieh Tzu and understand how they are being used today by modern Eastern and Western teachers we can begin to see what the

Western form of Taoism holds for us. The real proof of how these practices will work for us is in how well they work in our own daily lives, both individually and collectively. The simple and practical Taoist ways of doing and being teach us to cultivate our spiritual and physical gardens so we can grow into radiant, healthy and joyful beings.

As one of my teachers, Hui Xian Chen, has said:

> For me, I have not only learned from my masters but the most important way I have learned is from the people around me. The students, friends, children, even the trees and flowers. Sometimes I look at the flowers. They never charge me anything to look at them. They are so generous. The sun is so generous, passing its light to all people, poor or sick, rich, it does not matter who. If you are standing in the sun the sun is shining upon you, so generous. The wind, the rain, all of nature, so selfless. Can we be that selfless? We are not. If we can learn from the universe itself to become selfless, then we have attained Tao.

The way to self knowledge often seems long and arduous, when it can be simple and pragmatic. The way of Tao is a simple yet sublime combination of down-to-earth practicality and the ability to soar among the clouds on the backs of dragons. With a little practice and a lot of humility and patience, each one of us can one day count ourselves among the sages that Lao Tzu described so long ago:

> Therefore wise men embrace the one
> And set an example to all.
> Not putting on a display,
> They shine forth.
> Not justifying themselves,
> They are distinguished.
> Not boasting,
> They receive recognition.
> Not bragging
> They never falter.
> They do not quarrel,
> So no one quarrels with them.
> Therefore the ancients say,
> "Yield and overcome."
> Is that an empty saying?
> Be really whole,
> And all things will come to you.
>   (Chapter 22)

I

Taoism 101

What Is Tao?

The Tao has reality and evidence, but no action and no form. It may be transmitted but cannot be received. It may be attained but cannot be seen. It exists by and through itself. It existed before Heaven and earth, and indeed for all eternity.
Joseph Needham

What gives life to all creation and is itself inexhaustible — that is Tao.
Joseph Needham

It is the unmanifest potentiality from which all manifestations proceed.
Hua-Ching Ni

Tao is the everlasting rhythm of life, the unity of the polarity of non-being and being.
Ellen M. Chen

Tao is the pointing finger and, at the same time, the direction.
Hua-Ching Ni

Something mysteriously formed,
Born before heaven and earth.
In the silence and the void,
Standing alone and unchanging,
Ever present and in motion.
Perhaps it is the mother of ten thousand things.

I do not know its name.
Call it Tao.

Tao Te Ching

"The Tao that can be told is not the eternal Tao." So begins the *Tao Te Ching (Dow De Jing)* of Lao Tzu, written some 2,500 years ago. "I do not know its name, so I call it Tao. If you insist on a description, I may call it vast, active, moving in great cycles."

How then, to describe the indescribable? How to fit into words that which is beyond words? The Tao can only be pointed to, or referred to, say the ancient sages. It cannot be held, only experienced. It cannot be touched, only felt. It cannot be seen, only glimpsed with the inner eye.

As we see by the quotes at the beginning of the chapter, there are many ways of talking *about* Tao, but, like trying to describe the taste of chocolate to someone who has never had it, one can only approximate. Imagine then, trying to describe the be all and end all of existence. Lao Tzu began the *Tao Te Ching* by saying that the Tao itself cannot even be talked about—though he did manage to come up with a little over five thousand characters after that! What he actually meant was that to try to fit the Tao into a neatly packaged definition for once and for all is impossible, for in reality, Tao is something quite beyond all puny definitions and categories.

The word Tao (Dow), has many translations. It is an elusive word, meaning much more than can be explained. It has been called the Law or the Way or simply All That Is. Some Christian writers have even translated it as God, though it certainly does not mean the personal, judgmental deity we in the West usually think of as God.

Tao is at once the universal pageant of the constellations and the budding of each new leaf in the spring. It is the constant round of life and death and all that falls between. It resides in us as we reside in it. It is the source as well as the end of our being. It neither judges nor condemns but continually blesses, in all moments, an unending cycle of change and renewal.

Tao is what has always been and always will be, regardless of whether we humans blow ourselves into the astral. It actually has no need of us yet continually and forever sustains us. Alan Watts once wrote:

The order to Tao is not an obedience to anything else. As Chuang-tzu says, 'It exists by and through itself,' it is *sui generes* (self generating), *tzu-jan* (of itself so), and has the property of that forgotten attribute of God called aseity—that which is (by) se (itself).

Tao, then, is the Way, as in direction, as in manner, source, destination, purpose, and process. In discovering and exploring Tao the process and the destination are one and the same. John Blofeld says that in Chinese thought "the notion of a Supreme Being, so essential to Western religions, is replaced by that of a *Supreme State of Being*, an impersonal perfection from which all beings, including man, are separated only by delusion."

In other words, this Supreme State of Being is not some unattainable something "out there," far removed from the mundane affairs of humankind, but rather something that we too are integrally a part of. After all, it is much harder to identify with a wrathful, personified deity or even a perfect, shining glory of a deity than something so simple, so natural, so all encompassing as Tao. As Alan Watts said, "It may reign but it does not rule. It is the pattern of things but not the enforced."

The Tao itself does not judge, it does not condemn, it does not punish. Rather we ourselves, in our refusal to go along with its majestic flow, punish ourselves and cause ourselves all sorts of worries and problems. I like to think of it as a giant celestial merry-go-round. Around and around it goes, in its great and heavenly way. It is up to us to either jump on and ride in the direction it is already turning, or to attempt to jump on the other way. Of course, if we do that, we sooner or later get thrown off and land on our faces in the mud! As Lao Tzu says, whatever goes against the Tao comes to an early end. This is not a punishment or a judgment. It simply is the way things are. Spit into the wind and you receive it back into your face. Simple, natural.

But just think of the vast amount of whirling energy that is contained in that effortlessly revolving merry-go-round. And just imagine tapping into that energy, that force, by simply finding our own place on that wheel and going for the ride. When we are going along with the flow or direction of the Tao, or the natural flow, we derive great impetus and direction. It is like having the wind against our backs, filling our sails. We feel we can doing anything and everything our hearts desire. But try to go against it and once again we land on our faces in the mud.

It is in finding just the right way to jump aboard, the right timing, the right position, that is the tricky part. And that's just what this book is about.

What, Then, Is Taoism?

...a unique and extremely interesting combination of philosophy and religion, incorporating also 'proto' science and magic.
Joseph Needham

Taoism represents everything which is spontaneous, imaginative, private, unconventional...
A.C. Graham

A Taoist laughs at social conventions, and eludes or adapts himself to them.
Lieh Tzu

Taoism is not an "ism." It is also not an ideology, or a New Age movement. It is a *living philosophy*. It is a way of thinking, a way of looking at life, a way of being—being *with* change rather than *against* it. Life is made up of cycles, say the Taoists, cycle upon cycle. The only constant is change. Change is inescapable. We have no control over it. The only thing we have control over is our own responses to the changes life has to offer. For really, what else *can* we do?

Actually, there's plenty we can do. Rant and rave, complain, whine, procrastinate, fight back, resist. But to what avail? To resist only weakens us. To the Taoist, resistance is a joke. It is utterly futile and without honor. To resist only makes that which we are resisting stronger. Lao Tzu speaks over and over again of the principle of the soft overcoming the hard, the weak overcoming the strong.

Yield and overcome;
Bend and be straight;
Empty and be full;
Wear out and be new;
Have little and gain.

Later on he says:

The softest thing in the universe
Overcomes the hardest thing in the universe.

In yielding we can find strength and succor and in softness we can find a way to overcome even the worst tribulations. What we are talking about here is not a mushy, weak kind of softness, but a resilient, *decisive* softness, the springy softness of the bamboo which bends and springs back in contrast to the hard and stiff oak which is blown down in a hard wind.

Lao Tzu describes a Taoist as the one who sees simplicity in the complicated and achieves greatness in little things. He or she is dedicated to discovering the dance of the cosmos in the passing of each season as well as the passing of each precious moment in our lives. Lao Tzu calls him the sage; Chuang Tzu calls him the True Man (or woman). He says:

> Those who seek for and follow (the Tao) are strong of body, clear of mind, and sharp of sight and hearing. They do not load their mind with anxieties, and are flexible in their adjustment to external conditions.

Taoism was already long established when Lao Tzu wrote the *Tao Te Ching*. It originated in the ancient shamanic roots of Chinese civilization. Many of the practices and attitudes toward life were already established before Lao Tzu's time. He did, however, bring a much more philosophical bent to traditional Taoist teachings. As a matter of fact, this path was not even called "Taoism." Indeed, it was not called anything. It was only much later when Buddhism came to China and found royal favor that Taoism came to be called by that name. This was also when Taoism diverged from being a strictly philosophical path to a religious one, complete with liturgy, priests and even a Taoist pope!

Taoism has a long long history, stretching back to the Yellow Emperor (Huang Ti) who is said to have reigned during the middle of the third millennium BCE. It continues down through the sages such as Lao Tzu, Chuang Tzu, Ko Hong, Lu Dong-bin and countless other "invisible" sages, both men and women who have carried on the ancient traditions and created new practices even up to today.

The original form of Taoism, and the form that this book is most concerned with, is sometimes called philosophical Taoism or classical Taoism. For many centuries Taoism was an informal way of life, a way followed by peasant, farmer and gentleman philosopher and artist. It was a way of deep reflection and of learning from Nature, considered the highest teacher. Followers of the Way studied the stars in the heavens and the energy that lies deep within the earth. They meditated upon the energy flow within their own bodies and mapped out the roads and paths it traveled upon. They felt no need for official temples and liturgy. Each man and woman was their own priest. The connection with the divine or Tao was the sacred trust of each individual.

Then, as Eva Wong tells us:

> The history of Taoism took an interesting turn between the first and seventh centuries CE: a form of Taoism that combined magic and devotion emerged. Under the influence of a charismatic spiritual leader, Chang Tao-ling, Taoism became a religion.

Today one can visit Taoist temples in China, such as the famous White Clouds temple in Beijing and see crowds of devotees lighting clouds of incense and bowing down to statues of fierce looking gods in order to have "a good life" or for blessings in a new business enterprise. The Taoist canon consists of thousands of volumes and monks and nuns perform services complete with chanting, singing, exorcisms and talisman making.

Many of these monks and nuns are true students of the Way. They practice self cultivation very seriously and perform rites and rituals for pilgrims and tourists while understanding that the true Tao is not contained in any religious box.

Most Chinese people today view Taoism as just another old fashioned religion. The Taoism that I believe will take root in the West is not that religious form. It is instead a non-religious, deeply personal form of Taoism that speaks to the Westerner as deeply and richly as the Chinese.

As we shall see, Chinese medicine, qigong, tai ji, internal alchemy, energy meditation, all of these have their roots in the Taoism of Lao Tzu and Chuang Tzu and the ancient achieved ones. It is a form of Taoism that can be approached by anyone.

It is a belief in life, a belief in the glorious procession of each unfolding moment. It is a deeply spiritual but decidedly non-religious way of life. It involves introspection, balance, emotional and spiritual independence and responsibility and a deep awareness and connection to the Earth and all other life forms. It requires an understanding of how energy works in the body and how to treat illness in a safe, non-invasive way while teaching practical ways of maintaining health and avoiding disease and discomfort. Taoist meditation techniques help the practitioner enter deeper or more expansive levels of wakefulness and inner strength. But most of all it is a simple, natural, practical way of being in our bodies and our psyches and sharing that being with all other life forms we come into contact with.

Taoists believe in the divinity, specialness and deep down holiness of each individual, including themselves. As Hua-Ching Ni, a contemporary Taoist master, tells us, "An undistorted human life is the real model of all universal truth." The Taoist seeks to dig deep under all the layers of cultural and psychological silt that has accumulated in us humans over the millennia and bring forth the shining pearl that lies beneath. As Hua-Ching Ni says:

Ordinary religions can turn you into a pole; the naked electric pole on the side of the busy street, stark and barren, whereas Tao makes you sprout, blossom, and yield fruit as you sway and dance in the breeze of life.

So What Does This Have To Do With Me?

The simplest actions and the simplest language are needed to develop ourselves spiritually and present the whole truth.
Hua-Ching Ni

When people say they're looking for the meaning of life, what they're really looking for is a deep experience of it.
Joseph Campbell

He who understands the Way is certain to have command of basic principles. He who has command of basic principles is certain to know how to deal with circumstances. And he who knows how to deal with circumstances will not allow things to do him harm. When a man has perfect virtue (te), fire cannot burn him, water cannot drown him, cold and heat cannot affect him, birds and beasts cannot injure him.
Alan Watts

The modern world bombards us on every side with sensory, emotional, and psychological impressions. We often feel alone and cut off from our foundations, both spiritually and emotionally. For most of us, "reality" consists of spoon-size treatments of other people's lives fed to us in a steady diet by newspapers, radio and especially television. Everyone's life problems are solved in one half hour to one hour segments, including commercials. We feel disappointed and inferior if we are not able to do the same with our life problems and challenges.

Most modern religions emphasize the basic separation between creator and creation. God is somewhere "out there" and is to be supplicated, placated and feared. This intensifies our feelings of alienation, making them more unbearable. To use an economic term, we are heading into a state of spiritual bankruptcy. This is reflected in the ever deeper and wider range of psychological disturbances we see all around us. The "village idiot" has multiplied many times and is now living on the streets with nowhere to go. Carl Jung, writing in 1933, said, "Much of the evil in the world is due to the fact that man in general is hopelessly unconscious."

He realized that many psychological disturbances of modern humankind are actually a spiritual problem. We in the West have been cut off from our spiritual roots. And in the process, says Jung, "science has destroyed even the refuge of the inner life. What was once a sheltering haven has become a place of terror." "Modern man is solitary," he says, and "is so of necessity and at all times, for every step toward a fuller consciousness of the present removes him further from his original participation with the mass of men—submersion in a common unconsciousness."

Why has this happened? Why are modern men and women increasingly alienated from themselves and each other and seemingly from the rest of humanity? The Book of Genesis describes how Adam and Eve, the primordial man and woman, ate the fruit of the tree of knowledge and were consequently forced out of the Garden of Eden, doomed to live a life cursed and filled with pain and travail. Just what is this tree that caused such grave consequences for poor Adam and Eve? It is the tree of the knowledge of good and evil (or yin and yang, as the Taoist would say). It is the knowledge of opposite and complementary conditions and forces. The serpent, as the temptor, says to Eve that "God doth know that in the day ye eateth thereof, then your eyes shall be opened and ye shall be as gods, knowing good and evil." (Genesis 3:5)

Of course once they are found out they are cast out of paradise. Eve is told she shall henceforth deliver her children in sorrow and shall be ruled over by her husband, setting the scene for male domination for the next four thousand years. Adam is told he shall eat sorrow for all the days of his life. Not only that but the very ground under them will be cursed! All in all, things look pretty grim for humankind from this time forth. And while most of us today know that many stories of the Bible are myth and allegory, there are still plenty of people who believe these stories are literally true and are bound and determined to live out their days in sorrow and suffering, just as God commanded Adam to do.

To Taoists, however, this is absurd. The knowledge of good and evil or self knowledge is the right and legacy of every individual. Hua-Ching Ni says:

Don't let anyone tell you that you cannot know the truth for yourself or that you cannot achieve yourself spiritually without being tied to a temple or church. You were not born a spiritual slave. You are the authority who distinguishes what is true and untrue, spiritual and unspiritual.

It is so easy to just let spiritual or temporal authority figures tell us what to believe and how to live our lives. It is much easier than consciously choosing the journey of self discovery and self knowledge, a journey which can be very rocky indeed. In the immortal *Brothers Karamazov*, Doestoevsky relates the story of how Christ, when he returns to earth in the Middle Ages, is snatched immediately by the Grand Inquisitor and thrown into a dungeon. There he is told that his presence is not needed, that the Grand Inquisitor has everything under control. People *like* being told what to believe and how to live their lives. They don't need some upstart to stir things up. Christ's gift of spiritual freedom is not welcome here, the Inquisitor tells him. Not only do the people have no use for it, they would not know what to do with it if they had it. It would only be a problem and a burden to them. He then has Christ killed again.

What Doestoevsky was talking about then is still true today. Most people *would* rather be told what to believe in and how to live their lives in that belief. They don't want the dubious and highly dangerous gift of spiritual freedom any more than did the people of the Middle Ages. Wilhem Reich wrote about the killing of Christ, in which he posited that Christ has been crucified continuously for two thousand years. He is crucified every time we submerge and deny the Christ within us, that part of us that represents the love of life, of discovery, of ever evolving creativity, or our own undeniable divinity.

Again, to Taoists this is all quite absurd. Taoists, like many primal people, believe that *everything* is sacred, not just musty old "holy" books or special buildings or even special people whose job it is to act as intermediaries between the sacred and the profane. To the followers of the Way there is no difference between the sacred and the profane. There is no escaping Tao or sacredness. It is contained within everything as everything is contained within it.

We are still in the garden of Eden! Or as Christ put it, "Heaven is at hand." Just look around at the amazing variety of life that is going on around us all the time, in all its splendiferous color and shape and form. Webs of energy connect us all; trees sway rhythmically in the breeze high over our heads; water runs merrily or sedately over stones and sand, forming ripples and eddies and making delicious music; grasses and flowers grow boisterously, seductively, whether we even care or not. The rich panoply of life goes on all around us, always, endlessly.

You too are a unique and wonderful creation all your own. Feel the blood rushing through your veins as your heart pumps continuously and obligingly. Your lungs breathe effortlessly in and out, drawing rich oxygen and *qi* energy. Your eyes scan the page, deciphering the little blobs of black on white, while your marvelous brain interprets them to your consciousness. Your every cell hums with life, with energy, with consciousness. And who knows what further adventures await us when we tire of these bodies and leave them behind, setting our spirits adrift into the arms of the great and loving Tao?

Wake up and smell the miraculous fragrance of your own life and of all the life forms around you! The very richness of existence is contained in all that you know and are and all that you wish to know and be. Accept it into your consciousness, your own expression of the Tao.

As Taoists, we are artists of life. We are creators of our own masterpieces, directors of our own movies, writers of our own stories. We are not afraid to ask for help, but in doing so, we do it with pride, with humbleness, with sincerity, not as "worms" or "wretches" but as upright free individuals, invested in truth and learning, ever growing, ever renewed. We take responsibility for our own emotions, for our own relationships, for our own habits, for our own destiny. We are all made of the same "stuff," a combination of the divine and the organic. We are all atomically equal! We all want to be loved and to love. We all want to be happy and to be able to give happiness to others. We all want to be safe, to be whole, to be healthy. And that is our right, our divine inalienable right. We let no man or woman take that away from us through fear or guilt or intimidation.

We take responsibility for our own health. We take care of and treat our bodies in a healthy and balanced manner. We take responsibility for our own sexuality. We do not treat it as a weapon or a means of subjugation. We take responsibility for our own spirituality, for our own self cultivation. We nurture and weed our own spiritual gardens and reap the bountiful harvest. We take responsibility for our own emotional independence, not clinging to others or allowing others to cling to us in an unhealthy manner. We take responsibility for our own psyches. We do not trash them or twist them into unnatural shapes for the benefit of others or for our own immature needs.

And lastly, we take responsibility for our own consciousness, our own part of the dance, our own piece of the great cosmic puzzle. We respect ourselves and do not allow ourselves to be used in an unhealthy way by the ones we love, and in turn we do not use them in the same manner. We respect our origin and we honor our true selves, free of petty distractions and fears. We respect and honor the true self of everyone around us, and in that respect and honoring we shine forth as the true sacred and strong beings that we are.

Chapter Sources

Joseph Needham, *Science and Civilization in China*
Hua-Ching Ni, *The Gentle Path of Spiritual Progress*
Ellen M. Chen, *Tao Te Ching*
Gia Fu Feng & Jane English, *Tao Te Ching*
Eva Wong, *The Shambhala Guide toTaoism*
Alan Watts, *The Watercourse Way*
John Blofeld, *Taoism, The Road to Immortality*
A.C. Graham, *The Book of Lieh-Tzu*
Clae Waltham, *Chuang Tzu: Genius of the Absurd*
Hua-Ching Ni, *Tao: The Subtle Universal Law and the Integral Way of Life*
Hua-Ching Ni, *The Way of Integral Life*
Carl Jung, *Modern Man In Search of a Soul*

2

Lao Tzu and
the Tao Te Ching

The Tao Te Ching may be taken as a manual of advice on government, or as a book of natural philosophy, or as a compendium of metaphysical and mystical wisdom.
        Alan Watts

There is no other book so objective and undemanding in its expression of the natural truth.
        Hua-Ching Ni

The Tao Te Ching as a religious text preaches peace between humans and the natural world and thereby peace among humans.
        Ellen M. Chen

Just how Lao Tzu came to write the immortal *Tao Te Ching* is lost in the mists of time, but the story generally told is so charming that even if it were not true I think it bears repeating. And, as with any legend, there is always a kernel of truth that speaks to us.

Lao Tzu (or Lao Tan or simply the Old Boy) labored in the Chinese imperial capital of Loyang, first as palace secretary, then as keeper of the archives for the court of Chou around 2,500 years ago.

The Chou dynasty had been a long and creative one, but as time went on it became corrupt and decadent. China was entering into what was later called the Warring States Period. It was a time when the old code of honor and chivalry, much like the Knights of the Round Table, was dying out. No longer were battles fought by favorites in an honor-able and gentlemanly way. Nor did generals and armies wait for each other to deploy in an equally advantageous fashion before commencing battle. Now brutal annihilation led the day. Armies attacked each other indiscriminately, hacking the enemy to death by the thousands.

The peasants were caught in the middle. Rampaging armies crossed and recrossed their fields and farms, taking whatever they wished, forcibly conscripting the young men and often raping the young women. Power mad nobles scrambled for authority in the capital, using subterfuge and intrigue. Seemingly no one was safe in those mad times.

Is it any wonder that a philosopher and lover of life and Tao should decide to leave all the carnage and horror and enter the wilderness? This is apparently what Lao Tzu did. Taking no students or devotees and riding a water buffalo, a sure footed if plodding beast, he left the capital and headed for the western wilderness. When he reached the frontier border gate to the state of Ch'in, gatekeeper Wen-shihi, a friend and student, implored him to "at least leave a little something behind in the form of the written word so that your teachings will not be lost." In two days time Lao Tzu composed a little book in verse of slightly over five thousand characters, expounding the philosophy of Tao. He then mounted his noble steed and headed off into the mountains, never to be seen again!

And so we are left with this marvelous and wonderfully multi-layered book. Since then countless translations and commentaries have been made on the *Tao Te Ching*. As a matter of fact, it is the most widely translated book in the world after the Bible though it is certainly much shorter. Part of its appeal and value is that it can be understood on so many different levels. It is a poetic treatise on the philosophy of Tao, already ancient in Lao Tzu's time (he was not, as many authors have erroneously claimed, the originator of Taoism, though he was certainly one of its most brilliant expounders). It can be read as a manual of government, with its advice to the sagely ruler, or it can be read as a manual on enlightenment or self governance. It is written in a simple straightforward style and can be read over and over again, each time yielding new gems of wisdom and guidance. As the student of the Way journeys further and deeper, so too will the *Tao Te Ching* reveal layer upon layer of meaning.

Unfortunately it is extremely difficult to translate. It was written in archaic Chinese which has neither active or passive tense, no singular or plural, no case, no person, no tense and no mood. Indeed, as Holmes Welch wrote, "while some texts are more corrupt, some more archaic, and some more esoteric, no text—certainly none of comparable importance—so nicely combines vagueness with all these difficulties."

This being the case, there are as many individual translations as there are differences of opinion or understanding of just what Lao Tzu was saying. There are English translations from the 1940s that translate Tao as God, personifying the impersonifiable. Modern Chinese have even translated it into Marxist terms by having Lao Tzu speak out in support of Communist ideology! There are also many "pop" versions, with New Age or even psychological overtones.

No matter; the main thing is to find a version that speaks to your own heart. Compare several versions and see which one makes the most sense to you. Then read it slowly and often. The more you practice self cultivation and the more experienced you become both in Taoism and in life itself, the more ways you will experience the *Tao Te Ching*. There are many ways Lao Tzu's words can assist you. They will speak to you in different voices and different styles. As you study them closely and begin to apply Taoist principles to your life, you will begin to grow and prosper spiritually and emotionally. Again and again we will be quoting from this invaluable book throughout this work. Take this book to heart and you will see for yourself the value of the Old Boy's advice.

A fair number of authors and translators claim there was no such person as Lao Tzu, and that the *Tao Te Ching* was either written by someone else or is a compilation of several people's writings. It is very hard to say with any confidence that an actual person named Lao Tzu existed. It is too far back in time and Chinese records are often difficult to understand or verify. I prefer to assume such a marvelously humble and witty man as Lao Tzu indeed wrote the *Tao Te Ching*, exactly as the legend is told. No matter—whether or not Lao Tzu existed is of little importance. The work stands for itself. The *Tao Te Ching* has stood the test of time and continues to inspire and teach us today as it did 2,500 years ago.

Because this kind of work was traditionally known by the author's name, the *Tao Te Ching* was originally called the *Lao Tzu*. It wasn't until five or six hundred years later that the collection of writings came to be known as the *Tao Te Ching*. The title itself receives many translations. *The Canon of Tao and Te* (Chen), *The Way and Its Power* (Waley), *The Way and Integrity Classic* (Mair), *The Book of Tao* (Yutang), *The Book of the Way and Its Power* (Watts) are but a few of the titles Lao Tzu's work has been given in English.

Ching means book or work or sacred book. It puts the work into an honored position. *Tao* we have already talked about. *Te* is another problematic word, meaning different things to different people. To many it means virtue, but virtue in a slightly different sense than the Christian one. Hua-Ching Ni calls it "the creative power originating from the nature of the universe." Alan Watts calls te "the realization or expression of the Tao in actual living." He explains that "this is not virtue in the sense of moral rectitude."

Te has also been translated as power or personal power. It is a power that we are all born with but few of us develop. Part of self cultivation is to develop and enhance our te. In ancient times it was thought that emperors and other nobility had more te than the common people, though they too had to observe special rites and rituals to preserve and enhance it. Mountains and other high places were also thought to have great amounts of natural te and people climbed them at special times, such as on the ninth day of the ninth month, to absorb some of the most beneficial te.

The whole natural world was thought to contain te. Rocks, plants, animals—all contained their own source of divine power or te. Other cultures have had similar beliefs. The *orenda* or *wakan* of the Native Americans, the *pneuma* of the Greeks, and the "holy spark" of the Hasidim are all examples of this amorphous yet powerful substance. It is a kind of indwelling presence that all life forms share, similar to qi (chi).

Lao Tzu, in his great work, has shown us examples of how we may not only enhance but extend and build our own te or natural virtue. The *Tao Te Ching* has many examples of how this is done, and they will be explained throughout this book. Suffice it to say that the *Tao Te Ching* can be used as a handbook to protect and build your own sense of selfhood and sovereignty.

Eternal truth is very simple and very clear and does not come with any emotional or psychological baggage or attachments. The *Tao Te Ching* is a perfect example of eternal truth given in a clear, simple and concise way. You don't have to follow a guru or leader or join any religion to be able to use it effectively. Just use your own natural discrimination, apply it to your life and you will reap the benefits.

Chapter Sources

Alan Watts, *The Watercourse Way*
Hua-Ching Ni,*The Gentle Path of Spiritual Progress*
Gia-Fu Feng & Jane English, *Tao Te Ching*
Ellen M. Chen, *Tao Te Ching*
Holmes Welch, *Taoism, The Parting of the Way*

3

A Wandering Taoist

The cold wind blowing off the western desert ruffled the beard of the old man riding slowly atop the water buffalo. It whipped 'round his traveling cloak and made him shiver deep within his robes. He tried wrapping the cloak a little tighter around his shoulders but it did him little good. It was a bad time of the year for traveling, but that could not be helped. The stolid beast plodded on slowly toward the frontier. A horse would have been faster, but this beast was steadier, more sure-footed in the mountains and ate very little. He supposed it was a bit of reverse vanity that prompted him to travel on so humble a mount, the last vestige of the once proud royal archivist.

Lao Tan was leaving his post and his life in court behind him and heading toward the western frontier. Life in the capital had been going from bad to worse. In fact, as far as he was concerned, the whole society was falling apart. The court intrigue nauseated him, the constant political maneuvering gave him a headache, and it seemed as though cynicism was trickling down even into the lower classes. The tradesmen and shopkeepers were far more interested in making money than in being of good service. Even the farmers, the bedrock of civilization, were showing signs of dissatisfaction and doubt about their own lives.

Everywhere he looked Lao Tan saw signs that society was askew. It seemed to him that the Way had truly been lost and that things were only going to get worse. Even his students had become cynical, more interested in acquiring mystical powers than simply learning how to live in accord with the eternal Way, as if there were anything more powerful than that.

Armies were massing all along the borders of the various fiefs, ready to go at each other's throats at a moment's notice. And no longer were there chivalrous knights errant as in days past, seeking to redress the wrongs suffered by the weak at the hands of the rapacious strong. The ancient rules of combat in which battles were fought by favorites, thus avoiding needless bloodshed, were being ignored. Now, armies went at each other in wholesale slaughter, while the poor peasants whose lands they ravaged in battle suffered the loss of their crops, their sons and even their daughters to the bloodthirsty soldiers.

All in all, it had seemed like a good time to leave the festering swamp that society had become and head into the wilderness to pass his days in contemplation of the Way. So he had said good-bye to his students and his position, and since his wife had left this world of dust years before, he mounted his sturdy buffalo alone and slowly plodded toward the setting sun.

At the end of the day he reached the outermost gate of the kingdom. He slowly and stiffly dismounted and turned to the gatekeeper who had come out of his tiny hut to greet him. Wen-shih was a long-time friend and student and was about as old as Lao Tan himself.

"Master Lao," he said, coming forward, his wrinkled face breaking into a broad smile. "It's so good of you to visit. Are you on a vacation from the capital?"

"No," answered Lao Tan, "I'm afraid I'm done with all that. I am on my way out there." He pointed to the vast desert on the other side of the pass.

Wen-shih frowned. "But that way is very hard, and may even mean your death."

"No matter," said Lao Tan. "It is time for me to leave my old life behind and see what the Tao has in store for me."

Later, after a simple but delicious meal, Lao Tan and his friend sat by the fire and listened to the night sounds around them.

"Master Lao," began Wen-shih, "if you are really going, never to return, I beg you to please write something for your students so they may have some of your wisdom to refer to in the troubled times ahead."

"I am afraid that if they did not hear me when I was actually speaking to them, they surely will not listen to mere words on paper," answered Lao Tan.

"But," entreated Wen-shih, "if things are really getting as bad as you say, then we will surely be in need of whatever wisdom you can leave us."

"I dislike writing things down," answered Lao Tan, getting up and stretching. "I feel there is really no way to convey the immensity of the Way in simple words, no matter how clever or polished. Now I must go to bed, old friend. I will be leaving at first light."

Before going to bed, Lao Tan sat awhile, thinking over what Wen-shih had said. He did feel a little guilty about leaving his students and friends back at the capital. Perhaps writing a few lines would not be such a bad thing after all. It might even help him formulate his thoughts a little better in his own mind. He got out his writing implements and began mixing his ink. Then, with his brush poised over a long strip of bamboo, he stopped.

How could he possibly put into words the immensity and depth of the Way? How could he, in a few lines, bring forth all that he had experienced and learned in a lifetime of seeking the great and sublime Tao? For a moment the thought overwhelmed him. But even though he was quitting this sad and misguided world, he felt responsible to the people who were struggling under the weight of fear and ignorance. If it was possible to leave behind a small token of his concern for them, he felt he had a duty to do what he could.

And so, after taking one deep breath "from the bottom of his heels," he put his brush to the bamboo and began to write.

"The Tao that can be described is not the eternal Tao.

The name that can be spoken is not the eternal name."

4

The Value of Worthlessness

*The most balanced person is not always recognized for what he is;
when you look at him, you will not see anything outstanding about him.*
Hua-Ching Ni

A simple, plain and natural life is essential spiritual completeness.
Hua-Ching Ni

*The joy for the Taoist is that things have no use, and the future is not
important.*
Alan Watts

*in straw sandals
and a belt of hemp
in a rush raincoat
dangling an old gourd ladle
half like a fisherman
half like a woodcutter
my head like a raspberry patch
and my face like a dump
I'll bear
your laughter.*
Yun-k'an Tzu

*Thirty spokes share the wheel's hub;
It is the center hole that makes it useful.
Shape clay into a vessel;
It is the space within that makes it useful.
Therefore profit comes from what is there;
Usefulness from what is not there.*
Chapter 11)

Once a man came to see Chuang Tzu and complained about a tree he owned. "It is huge," he said. "It covers my whole yard. It is very old and has been there for as long as anyone in the village can remember. Yet it is an ugly old thing. Its branches are so twisted and knotted that they are perfectly useless for timber. The wood is so hard it resists all axes and saws and cannot even be used for firewood. Hundreds of birds nest in it and all in all it is perfectly worthless."

"Ah," answered Chuang Tzu, "perhaps this troublesome tree of yours has some worth after all."

"But how can that be, you old faker!" cried the man.

"Think on it this way, honorable sir," said the sage, lightly stroking his whiskers. "You say the tree is of no use as lumber. It also cannot be chopped up for firewood. Think then, of how useful that has been for the tree. It surely would never have attained its great height and size if it had been more useful to the carpenter or the woodcutter. Why, it would have been cut down long ago, would it not?

"The trees that have straight, true trunks or the ones that have easily cut limbs are never allowed to grow to maturity. They, by their very nature of usefulness, are killed very quickly and are not allowed to flourish into their true prime.

"This tree of yours, did you not say it shielded the whole yard from the harsh sunlight?"

"Why, yes," replied the man.

"Well then, go and sit in its cool shade and rest from your labors. Let your children climb and play in its crooked limbs. And as for the birds, would they not build their nests somewhere else, perhaps in your roof, if they did not have the tree to live in? Besides, try to listen to their singing with a different ear and perhaps their music will begin to delight you.

"So too, my friend, it is with men and women. Those who would make ostentatious display of their great worth are all too quickly used up and thrown aside. But those who appear useless in the eyes of the world are allowed to live out their lives in peace. Thus they may be able to provide some small nourishment to those around them."

It is just this concept of the value of worthlessness that marks Taoism as a unique philosophy. "Profit," says the *Tao Te Ching*, "comes from what is there. Usefulness comes from what is not there." How different this way of thinking is from our modern world where one's worth depends on how bright one is or how attractive or how much one is able to accomplish, to produce!

In the face of this artificially high standard of worth, most people feel lacking. Our schools, our businesses, our streets are filled with people who feel they do not measure up. They do not feel they are worthy—of love, of respect, of happiness, of good fortune.

Chuang Tzu describes the "true man of old" as one who "did not mind being poor. He took no pride in his achievements. He made no plans. Thus he could commit an error and not regret it. He could succeed without being proud."

It is the intrinsic worthiness of being a human being, in all the most sublime and most inarticulate aspects, that gives us our worth, our special value. To look for it in outside achievements or in superficial and glamorous ways misses the point altogether. Our value as human beings, as emotional beings, as physical beings, as spiritual beings, resides deep within us, down in the place we all share, as children of the Tao.

Chuang Tzu also tells us about a hunchbacked man named Shu. It seems the poor man was so deformed that his chin rested on his navel, his shoulders rose up over his head, his top knot pointed to the sky, his organs were shoved together and his thigh bones were in line with his hips. But by washing clothes and sewing he was able to support himself.

Not content with that, he also winnowed and sifted grain and was able to make enough to support ten people. Also, when soldiers appeared in his village to press the men into service, they always passed over Shu. When work gangs were being formed for public works, he was exempt. And lastly, when the government gave out grain and wood to the needy, he always got more than anyone.

If this poor man, says Chuang Tzu, was able to support himself so ably, how much easier should it be for those of us whose deformities are those of the mind!

He then tells us about Ai Tai To, the ugliest man in his district. He was said to be so ugly he would scare anyone under heaven, yet young women who saw him told their parents they would rather be his concubine than other men's wives! Because he always went along with whatever anyone else said, he was never in the position of leader or ruler over anyone else. And though he never left his village and knew only what happened there, everyone regarded him highly.

The Duke of Ai heard about this remarkable man and, deciding that he must find out his secret, summoned him to the court. Indeed Ai Tai To was extremely ugly—even hideous—yet there was something about the man that he liked, even trusted. After spending some time with him, the Duke began giving Ai Tai To more and more responsibility in his government. At one point he offered him the the position of chief minister. Bashful, Ai Tai To hesitated as though he did not wish to take it. The Duke became so ashamed of himself before this humble yet wise man that he gave him the entire goverment of his realm. But in a short time Ai Tai To disappeared, leaving the Duke bereft and alone.

Shu and Ai Tai To, both deformed by the world's standards yet so in synch with the Tao, were not only able to live out their lives in peace and contentment but were able to inspire in others a feeling of trust and even love. Could it be that they were able to realize the worthiness of the seemingly worthless?

Thomas Merton quotes the Madman of Chu who says:

> The tree on the mountain height is its own enemy.
> The grease that feeds the light devours itself.
> The cinnamon tree is edible: so it is cut down!
> The lacquer tree is profitable: so they maim it.
> Every man knows how useful it is to be useful.
>
> No one seems to know
> How useful it is to be useless.

We all want to be useful. We all want to be thought of as worthy—of love, of respect, perhaps even of attention and riches. We would like to think of ourselves as being useful to those around us—our families, our communities, the people we work with. But who actually measures usefulness? Who is it that sets up the scales of worthiness? Who *decides* who is worthy and who is not?

Taoism teaches us that each one of us—man, woman, child; black, white, red, brown or yellow—is a unique and miraculous being, and each of us deserves love, respect and the chance to express ourselves *as* ourselves, in the most unique and natural way we can. Only in this way can we personally determine our usefulness, our worthiness, our own special sense of who and what we are.

Lao Tzu says:

> Better stop short than fill to the brim.
> Oversharpen the blade, and the edge will soon blunt.
> Amass a store of gold and jade, and no one can protect it.
> Claim wealth and titles, and disaster will follow.
> Retire when the work is done.
> This is the way of heaven.
>   (Chapter 9)

To overdo, to emphasize productivity, to oversharpen the blade is to invite disaster. When will the world acknowledge the worth of the mundane, the value of the ordinary, the utter preciousness of the commonplace?

This is the age of the celebrity, the superstar. No longer is a person satisfied with being merely competent or experienced at what she or he does, but now she must be the *best*, the *most* famous, the *most* successful, the most highly regarded.

Lao Tzu, after writing the *Tao Te Ching*, one of the most sublime and articulate books ever written, disappeared. He didn't stay around to become the famous author, the great teacher, the powerful guru or religious leader. He did his work and left for the wilderness—and was never heard from again!

Although he was a great teacher and philosopher, Chuang Tzu, too, preferred to remain a simple man. He tells the story about Hsu Yu, a fellow of such great wisdom that the Emperor Yao himself offered to step down from the dragon throne in his favor. Hsu Yu was so disgusted when he heard the offer that he not only refused but immediately ran to the river to wash out his ears! While he was there a boy came by, driving a team of oxen to the river to drink. The boy asked Hsu Yu why he was washing his ears out so thoroughly. Hsu Yu told him that the Emperor had offered to abdicate the throne to him, which made him feel so dirty he had to run right down to the river and wash out his ears.

Upon hearing this the boy started driving his oxen out of the water. Hsu Yu asked him why he was driving his animals out of the river when they hadn't finished drinking yet. The boy replied, "The filth from your ears is dirtying the river water. Do you think I want all that dirty water in my oxen's mouth?"

Taoism also gives close attention to cycles, those times when one is ahead, only the next day to be behind. One day everything goes well, the next, nothing works out. One day you're famous, beloved by the world, the next day you're a nobody. This is natural, say the Taoists; life is full of change. It encompasses each up and down and the all-too-brief moments in between. When we allow ourselves the space to be a nobody, to be willing to experience the down as well as the up days, we can come closest to being called men and women of Tao.

When we are willing to be worthless, we become worthy. As the ancient achieved ones explain, it is only in emptying ourselves of our mental and emotional baggage that we become fit to receive. This concept is illustrated by the famous story of the highly educated and somewhat arrogant gentleman who comes to visit the renowned master so that the sage can show him a few things he may not yet know.

"Please sit down and join me in some tea, esteemed sir," offers the old man.

They sit, and while the gentleman boasts about his education and recounts his accomplishments, the old man begins filling his guest's tea cup. As the gentleman rambles on, so too does the old man keep pouring tea into his cup until the tea overflows and begins running across the table and into the gentleman's lap.

What are you doing, you old dolt!" he shrieks, leaping up from his chair. "You're spilling tea everywhere. Can't you see that the cup is already full?"

The sage calmly stops pouring the tea and looks up at him. "You're mind sir, is much like this tea cup. I'm afraid it is already too full for me to be able to fit anything else into it. Else it will surely run over and spill everywhere."

So too must we be willing to empty our cups and become a *nobody*, to empty our minds and hearts of preconceived notions of knowledge and ideas of importance and accomplishment. To become a nobody is perhaps a greater accomplishment than to be a *somebody*. It seems in this day and age of mass communication and the fascination with celebrity that it is not so hard to become a somebody, if only for a day. The qualifications to become a somebody are getting slighter and slighter all the time. But to become a nobod—a happy, well balanced nobody—ah, *that* is a challenge!

To be a nobody in this world of "wannabe"somebodys is an aspiration worthy of the highest student. To be a nobody is to say "yes" to the natural order of being. To be a nobody is to acknowledge that we are precious and perfect in our imperfection, worthy in our worthlessness. To be a nobody is to say I am content and satisfied with who and what I am. To be a nobody is to blend in with the world around us in perfect naturalness and simplicity. To be a nobody is to give that precious part of ourselves, in a selfless and resolute manner. To be a nobody is to admit, to ourselves and to the world, that we are indeed linked with all the sages and, like them, we will continue to develop and grow and cultivate ourselves in a simple and natural manner. And lastly, to be a nobody is to redeem ourselves in our very emptiness, to be perfect vessels for Tao to manifest itself continually.

Perhaps then we may be able to become as useful in our worthlessness as that ancient gnarled tree.

Chapter Sources

Hua-Ching Ni, *The Taoist Inner View of the Universe
    and the Immortal Realm*
Alan Watts, *The Watercourse Way*
Jerome P. Seaton, *The Wine of Endless Life*
Gia-Fu Feng & Jane English, *Chuang Tzu, Inner Chapters*
Clae Waltham, *Chuang Tzu: Genius of the Absurd*
Thomas Merton, *The Way of Chuang Tzu*
Da Liu, *The Tao and Chinese Culture*

5

Down By the River

The old man sat on the muddy bank of the great river, fishing quietly and watching the water flow. He liked it here, out with the sun and the mosquitoes, his toes squishing delightfully in the mud, his bottom getting wet with the early morning dew. He didn't mind a little dampness. He just liked sitting by the river and watching the water flow by. His line trailed out into the water, though he used no bait. Whether or not he actually caught a fish was not important. The simple act of sitting by the river, toes in the mud, line dancing over the water, was enough for him.

The old man had been a philosopher and student of the Way for quite some time. He knew he was not popular with certain segments of society, those pedantic logicians and the like who used words as a screen to hide behind or else brandished them like weapons. His teaching had always been a bit convoluted and full of riddles, puns and a sublime sense of the ridiculous. As for arguments with other scholars and philosophers—he just wasn't interested. He often said that if two people argue and one wins and the other loses, does that mean one is right and the other wrong? Or are they both partly right and partly wrong? Or are both all right and also all wrong? Waiting for final answers is like waiting for nothing, he told his students. Look at everything in relation to the great Tao and leave differing viewpoints as they are. That's the way to live out one's life in peace and harmony.

He knew he was often laughed at behind his back, and sometimes to his face. So what? He didn't care! He knew what he knew and he also knew what he didn't know and that was enough for him. Still, his fame had spread lately and he was continually being bothered by people seeking the ultimate truth, as if such a thing could ever be conceptualized and put into plain words. Besides, it wasn't up to him to tell people the "ultimate truth." He could only share *his* truth, and even that changed from day to day, just like the ongoing cycles of the seasons.

No, he was better off here by the river, alone except for the mosquitoes and an occasional bird. He loved looking at the river and thinking about the great, unfolding Way and his place in it. He had learned
a lot just by sitting here and watching the water flow by. He noticed
that many people's energy flow was like water. Some people just had
little trickles, like a small creek. Other's energy was clogged and muddied, like a dammed up stream. Others' was wild and turbulent like a
river in the spring. Others' flowed serenely along, like the great river
in front of him. Still others' flowed fast and furious like the rapids he
knew were up river, then at other times it grew sluggish and heavy
like the part of the river that flowed past the village downstream. The
trick was to find a rhythm that suited one's self and try to stick to that.
It was far better to be harmonious and consistent than it was to change
one's flow every other day or even many times a day. He himself had
been quite turbulent in his youth, but a combination of self-cultivation
and suffering had changed that. Now he just liked to sit here, toes
squishing, line dancing, mind empty, bottom soaking, and enjoy the
day.

Suddenly he heard a commotion behind him. Two men were slid-
ing down the muddy bank toward him. They wore the insignia of
messengers for the local lord who lived on the other side of the river, in
a great castle. The old man had never seen this great lord, since the
lord did not condescend to travel among the common people. Years
ago the old man had lived in the capital and had known many such
men. They were mostly a very boring and irritating crowd, their energy stuck in their feet. They were the reason he had left the capital
long ago and retired to this small village by the river.

The two messengers, who wore costly robes of silk, were struggling to hold up their hems to avoid getting them muddied. They were
out of breath by the time they reached the old man, who sat with his
back to them.

"Honored sir," they panted. "Are you the one they call ———?"
They used an honorific title he had been given years ago at the capital
in recognition of his sagehood. He thought at first of denying it but
realized they already knew who he was when they first climbed down
the riverbank. They were only using a formality. He knew it all so well—
the empty, flowery phrases that fell from their tongues like rancid but-
ter.

Sighing, he got up slowly and turned to face them. "Yes," he answered. "I am that most unworthy person." He knew how to play the
game.

The two silken messengers looked at each other. Could this really be the great sage that their lord had sent them after? Why, he looked like a ragged fisherman! Yet there was something about his direct and piercing gaze that held them for a moment, like the sun coming out from behind a cloud. Then, just as suddenly, it was gone again and the old man stood before them, idly picking his nose.

"We have been sent by the great lord of this province to bid you come to his castle so he may humbly prostrate himself before you and beg of you to share some small part of your great wisdom with his lowly household."

What a crock! The old man knew just what would happen if he allowed himself to be led to the castle. Hours and hours of fawning and false modesty, to be followed by days and days of being a virtual prisoner, arguing with a dim-witted nobleman who had never had an original thought in his head. He would have to deal with whatever other "sages" the noble had ensconced there to argue philosophy in front of him. All his life he had dealt with those high-minded, long-winded Confucians who confused propriety and wisdom, duty and Tao, classism and true spiritual freedom. He wanted no more to do with them.

And the logicians were even worse. How they loved to confuse and conspire with endless torrents of words—words with no spirit, no real energy behind them, words which clouded the mind and induced a narcotic, hypnotic effect that numbed the mind to the true reality of the Way. How many endless hours had he already spent trying to get them to let go of their precious concepts and opinions and open themselves to the simple, unadorned truth of the integral and eternal Way?

No, he could not stomach any more of that. He had to find a way to turn them away without incurring the wrath of their great lord. Suddenly an idea came to him. "You have the shell of a ritual tortoise at the castle, do you not?"

The two messengers did not know what to say. This old man was a little abrupt. They had expected him to jump at the chance to be set up in the castle. After all, he would be paid well for his efforts and he would be wearing much finer clothing than the old rags he presently wore and be enveloped in much richer surroundings than this mosquito-infested, muddy riverbank.

"Yes," answered one of them, finally. "We do have a great and ancient tortoise shell which, as you most assuredly know, great sage, is used for divination at certain times of the year. "

The old man could imagine the pomp and circumstance of the divination ceremony: The ancient tortoise shell would be carried into the hall of divination between rows and rows of seated nobles and servants, stiff and formal. The procession would be accompanied by the ancient sing-song music of the Confucians, more irritating and less musical than the whining of the mosquitoes in his ear. Endless speeches and formal testimonials would follow. At last would come the ceremonial heating of the tortoise shell; the cracks which appeared on it could then be read. Would the year in question be good or bad for the great lord and his fief? The priests were not fools; they were not stupid enough to share bad tidings, even if they read them on the tortoise shell. The great lord would not want to know about the floods, the many farmers going hungry, the diseases and the pestilence that would be visited upon the common people that year. No, the great lord would want to hear how beneficent and wise he was, what a great ruler of men he was, what a generous and compassionate father to his people he was. The very thought of it made the old man want to vomit right there at the silken feet of the great lord's messengers.

"Well," he said, "what do you fellows think? I can see you are intelligent men. If the tortoise himself had been given the choice between being slaughtered for his shell to be venerated for hundreds of years or to be left along to drag his tail in the mud, what do you think the tortoise would have wanted?"

The two messengers looked at each other again. Was this some kind of test? They had been told that the old man was a bit odd, some even thought him crazy. They both decided to take their time in answering, just in case. Finally one of them took a deep breath and spoke. "I suppose," he said slowly, "that if it were truly up to the tortoise, why of course he would rather have been left alone to, as you say, drag his tail through the mud."

"Then that is precisely what I intend to do with mine," said the old man and abruptly turned his back on them, his muddy bottom winking obscenely. He gathered up his fishing line and trudged down the bank, singing an old folk song at the top of his lungs.

The messengers watched him for some time as he walked slowly away. What would they say to the great lord? They were not even sure themselves what had just happened. To think they had walked all this way and gotten muddy and mosquito bitten for this! It was true, they would tell their lord, the old man was crazy, not a sage, not a wise man. Just a crazy old man sitting on his ass in the mud.

6

The Wisdom of Foolishness
Chuang Tzu and Lieh Tzu

The humor, the sophistication, the literary genius and philosophical insight of Chuang Tzu are evident to anyone who samples his work.
Thomas Merton

(Chuang Tzu) advocated the nondirected method of participation in nature, a Way or learning the course of things, of developing a capacity to allow things to happen spontaneously, a living of life from one's subtle inward guidance.
Clae Waltham

Laotse smiled; Chuangtse laughed. Laotse taught; Chuangtse scoffed. Laotse praised the humble; Chuangtse lambasted the great.
Lin Yutang

Chuang Tzu, that sublime master of the ridiculous, is a major figure in classical Taoism. Born around 200 BCE, he came a little after Lao Tzu. Also, while Lao Tzu's writings are short, pithy, even poetic statements, Chuang Tzu's are voluminous and full of puns, riddles and outright jokes. He challenges the status quo at all times and maintains his right to live his own life the way he sees fit (as in the story of the sacred tortoise in the next chapter). Clae Waltham writes about him:

He spoke for a generation weary of hearing about benevolence and righteousness in the midst of slaughter. He advocated a return to simplicity in order to regain individuality. He rejected the mass behavior of man the bad animal, and urged a rediscovery of spontaneity. He believed that the only discipline was self-discipline. All that contained the possibility of good, all that was constructive, and all that was evolutionary, was summed up in the phrase 'the attainment of Tao.'

Chungliang Al Huang tells us that for most Chinese, Chuang Tzu "represents the best of what we admire in a person."

He is brilliant and mystical, philosophically pragmatic, witty and delightful, successful in being untainted by the need to succeed, and, most importantly, he is free. He is his own person, wandering through life like wind and water, enjoying its many delights without cumbersome attachments. The core of Chuang Tsu is this sense of ultimate freedom. He manages to exist quite sanely in the chaotic world, enjoying the best of humanity, without being dragged under. He seems to see through all the veil of human sufferings camouflaging the eternal truth.

In Chuang Tzu's writings we find advice on how to conduct ourselves in a simple, straightforward fashion, uncorrupted by society's strictures or by desperate attempts at fame and fortune. He sets forth description after description of the sage or The True Man. Here's how, in Gia-Fu Feng and Jane English's translation, he describes him:

The true man of old did not mind being poor. He took no pride in his achievements. He made no plans. Thus, he could commit an error and not regret it. He could succeed without being proud. Thus, he could climb mountains without fear, enter water without getting wet, and pass through fire unscathed. This is the knowledge that leads to Tao.
The true man of old slept without dreaming and woke without anxiety. His food was plain, and his breath was deep.

And further:

The true man of old knew nothing about loving life or hating death. When he was born, he felt no elation. When he entered death, there was no sorrow. Carefree he went. Carefree he came. That was all. He did not forget his beginning and he did not seek his end. He accepted what he was given with delight, and when it was gone, he gave it no more thought. This is called not using the mind against Tao and not using man to help heaven. Such was the true man.

This is a clear-cut primer for peace of mind and a balanced lifestyle. In Chuang Tzu's writings we see a man who pulled no punches and seemingly shrank from nothing, including criticism or even praise. Indeed, the idea of fame and fortune was an anathema to many Taoists, who viewed it with suspicion and even horror.

Besides the ability to play the fool when he felt it was needed, Chuang Tzu was also a formidable logician, though he used reason and logic in a peculiar way. One might even call it inside out reasoning. Victor Mair says "what logic there is in Chuang Tzu is directed against reason itself, in particular against the rational choice between one course of action and another."

An illustrative passage reads:

> To use one's fingers to demonstrate fingers not being fingers is not as good as using something else to demonstrate fingers not being fingers. Using horses is not as good as using something else to demonstrate horses not being horses. 'Heaven and earth' are like a finger, 'the ten thousand things' are like a horse.

Later on in the same chapter he says:

> A path is formed by walking on it. A thing has a name because of its being called something. Why is it like this? Because it is! Why is it not like that? Because it is not! Everything has its own nature and function.

See what I mean? Functional, practical! One might even venture to say reasonable! He ends this chapter by quoting the old story of the three monkeys, which illustrates the idea of "wracking your brain trying to unify things without knowing that they are already one."

A man had three monkeys. One day he tells them they will receive three acorns in the morning and four acorns in the evening. For some reason this angers the monkeys very much. "How dare you," they shout at him. "We will not stand for it!" So, thinking quickly, the man says, "Well then, I have taken your opinions into account and I have decided that you shall have four acorns in the morning and three in the evening." At this, the monkeys are happy, feeling they have put one over on their human master. The point is, of course, that they are still receiving exactly the same amount of acorns as in the beginning. It is only the appearance that has changed.

I think Chuang Tzu is telling us not to try to figure out the Tao, not to try to force one's own concept of oneness onto the Tao, and not to try to use reason or logic or any of the tools that we are used to using to make sense of the universe. Things are the way they are because they are! And they are not because they are not!

Mair says that "by mocking reason and delighting in the possibility of putting his message into words, the Taoist seems to withdraw beyond the reach of discussion and critics." Why do Taoists do this? Because they are not interested in playing mind games about who is more enlightened or deeper or higher than the next one. (Zen Buddhism, that wonderfully practical and simple, straightforward tradition of Japan, is actually a combination of Chan Buddhism and Taoism. The love of the spontaneous gesture, straight from the heart of the

Buddha Mind; the recognition of the importance of physical labor; the insistence of direct experience, outside of scripture and other "book learning" is all inspired by Taoism.)

Chuang Tzu says that "the Tao is hidden by partial understanding. The meaning of words is hidden by flowery rhetoric." Remember, Lao Tzu said the Tao that can be explained in words is not the true Tao. Anyone who tells you they can explain the universe and your place in it for you is off the track. They are just spouting *their* version of the truth. No one person or religion has a monopoly on the truth. Even Taoists would admit that there are as many versions of the truth or the Tao as there are living beings on this planet or any other. Certainly there are valuable guides and teachers along the way who can help us advance and gain greater knowledge, but to give up your spiritual sovereignty to someone else is a foolish thing to do. Listen to them, watch what they do, and use whatever applies to you. Take the best, then leave the rest.

Thomas Merton says of Chuang Tzu:

> Though he did not follow other men in their follies, he did not judge them severely—he knew that he had follies of his own, and had the good sense to accept the fact and enjoy it. In fact he saw that one basic characteristic of the sage is that he recognizes himself to be *as other men are*. He does not set himself apart from others and above them. And yet there is a difference; he differs *"in his heart"* from other men, since he is centered on Tao and not on himself. But "he does not know in what way he is different." He is also aware of his relatedness to others, his union with them but he does not "understand" this either. He merely lives it.

Chuang Tzu leaves us with a sense that all things are possible in the multiverse of Tao; by living it, we come closest to understanding and embodying it. The answers to all our questions are hidden everywhere, just outside our line of sight—that is, until we open our eyes a little wider and begin looking around us instead of just straight ahead. Then they jump out at us from everywhere, displaying themselves in all their stunning simplicity.

There are teachers everywhere, in all places. Chuang Tzu, Lieh Tzu and even Lao Tzu are just three of the vast number of Taoist teachers and masters who have shared their wisdom over numerous centuries. But true Taoist masters are experts at invisibility. They don't proclaim themselves to the world as enlightened beings. They don't run huge glossy ads in New Age magazines. They're not even recognizable at first glance. They could be living next door to you and you'd never know it until you learned to see with the eye of the heart (an old way of saying with the eye of discriminating consciousness).

It is thought that the *Book of Lieh Tzu* was not actually written by Lieh Tzu himself. A.C. Graham, in his excellent translation says:

> From its first maturity in the 3rd century B.C.E. we find references to a certain Lieh Tzu, who traveled by riding on the wind. His historicity is doubtful, and it is not even clear when he is supposed to have lived; some indications point to 600, others to 400 B.C.E. The book which carries his name is a collection of stories, sayings, and brief essays grouped in eight chapters, each loosely organized around a single theme.

And what a collection! Some parts are merely instruction, others are wild fantasy. Fantastic animals, tales of upside down worlds where people sleep during the daytime and work during the night, and obtuse philosophical meandering combine for an entertaining as well as enlightening journey.

Lieh Tzu says that much of what happens to us and how we react to it depends on our attitude. Eva Wong, in her version of Lieh Tzu says: "If we listen with a quiet mind and do not let our ideas distract us, we will understand others even before words are spoken."

In other words, since we really have no control over much of what happens to us, our strength lies in how we react to life's circumstances. As Eva Wong says:

> According to Lieh Tzu, fortune and misfortune and life and death come of their own without any direction or control from us or from a supreme being. Given this, why worry over things that we cannot do much about? Why try to predict what may happen and anticipate with anxiety?

Taoists must have originated the phrase "Shit happens." No matter how good we are, how often we meditate, how many hours of qigong we do, how clean our diet is, how clear we are with out emotion/thought patterns, sometimes things happen to us or around us that are difficult and challenging. When we have no control over our experiences, the only thing we *do* have control over is the way we react to them. This is a complete and very deep practice in itself, one that can take many years to develop. It is not for the faint-hearted.

One of Lieh Tzu's stories describes two men, one the owner of a large estate and the other a lowly worker on that estate. By day the worker toils unremittingly in the fields, falls to his bed exhausted at night and dreams that he is the owner enjoying a wonderful life, full of luxuries. Meanwhile the landowner spends his nights sweating and tossing through horrendous nightmares in which he is working in his own fields all day long. He awakens exhausted each morning.

In this story we see how the balance of the Tao is enacted in these two men's dreamlife. The lowly worker can deal with his lot because during the other half of his life he is enjoying the luxuries of being a rich man. On the other hand, the rich man is tortured at night while he experiences the hard life that his workers must live.

Eva Wong gives a wonderful description of Lieh Tzu:

Lieh-tzu lives in our world. He talks about experiences we can understand, he speaks about life and death, fortune and misfortune, gain and loss, things we are concerned with, and problems we want to solve in our lives. He talks about the mad race for wealth and renown and the hazards of seeking social recognition. He scorns social pressure and the empty pursuits of the rich and famous. He talks about friendship, human communication, dreams, reality, and learning. He speaks things we do not dare to speak of, but when we listen to him, we may smile, laugh, or nod in agreement. The awakening from ignorance is not rude but soft. It is as if someone gently shook us and woke us from a deep sleep.

One story tells of how Lieh Tzu was on his way to Chi but decided to turn back half way. He meets his friend and teacher Po-hun Wu-jen, who asks him why he has turned back.

"I was alarmed by something," says Lieh Tzu.

"What was it?" asks his friend.

Lieh Tzu explains that at every inn he ate he was served first.

Why is that such a prolem he is asked.

"When a man's inner integrity is not firm," says Lieh Tzu, "something oozes from his body and becomes an aura, which outside him presses on the hearts of others. It makes other men honor him more than his elders and betters, and gets him into difficulties."

He goes on to describe how the only motive of the innkeeper is to sell his wares and make his profit. If such a man as this values me so highly, think of how much worse it will be when the great lord finds out about him. "The prince of Chi will appoint me to some office, and insist that I fill it efficiently" he says, "this is what has alarmed me."

"An excellent way to look at it!" says Po-hun Wu-jen. "But even if you stay, other men will lay responsibilities on you."

Rather than being pleased that he is receiving so much special attention, Lieh Tzu is instead alarmed. Like Chuang Tzu, he has no interest in honors or official titles, believing they will get him into trouble in the world of political intrigue.

At another time, when Po-hun Wu-jen visits Lieh Tzu, he finds his doorway crowded with the shoes of visitors. When he turns to leave, Lieh Tzu sees him and runs after him and asks him if he has come to give him his blessing.

"Enough!" thunders Po-hun Wu-jen. "I told you confidentially that others would lay responsibilities on you, and it turns out that so they have."

He then says a very curious thing. "It is not that you are capable of allowing them to do it to you, you are incapable of preventing them. What use is it to you to have this effect on people, which is incompatible with your own peace? If you insist on having an effect, it will unsteady your basic self, and to no purpose."

In addition to felixiblity and humbleness, another uniquely Taoist trait is to be invisible. The ability to blend in with one's surroundings, spiritually as well as physically, is considered an art among traditional Taoists. Ostentation, bragging, being inordinately aware of one's accomplishments—all these are considered crass and not "of the Tao." Lao Tzu, Chuang Tzu and Lieh Tzu point out time and time again the dangers of spiritual materialism.

Instead, we are repeatedly reminded of the "true man of old," who is poetically described in the followed passage from John Blofeld:

> He is the eternal wanderer who tranquilly takes things as they come, putting forth energy when needed but inwardly relaxed. When things go well, he enjoys them to the full, though rather in the manner of someone charmed by an unexpected vista or primrose in a wood, who rejoices in their beauty for a little while, without the least desire to cling or to possess, and then passes on. When ills befall, he accepts them without repining, knowing full well there can be no up without down, no summer without winter, no growth without decay; besides, he is quick to discover beauty in the seemingly dreary and to find compensations in what to others might appear to be unmitigated ills.

Now let us leave these two unique gentlemen, with a tale from each. Both stories are about a cure of some kind. The first is from Chuang Tzu.

One day Duke Huan is hunting by a marsh and sees a ghost. Laying his hand upon his servant, he asks him if he has seen anything and is told that he has not.

The duke returns home, talking incoherently and becoming ill. After several days of this a man named Huang Tzu comes to see him and says, "Your Grace is hurting yourself. How could a ghost injure you?" He then goes on to describe how the fright the Duke has suffered has irritated his qi, which is making him ill.

The Duke then asks if there truly are ghosts and spirits.

Huang Tzu replies, "There are." He then describes various spirits and where they live, such as Ch-ieh, which hangs around furnaces; Lei-ting, who lives in dust heaps inside the door, and so on. He finally mentions the Wei-to who lives in marshes.

The Duke's interest perks up. "What is the Wei-to like?" he asks.

Huang Tzu tells him, "It is like the size of the hub of a chariot wheel and the length of the shaft. It wears a purple robe and red cap. It dislikes the rumbling noise of the chariot wheels; when it hears it, it puts both its hands to its head and stands up. He who sees it is likely to become the leader of all the other princes."

The honorable Duke bursts out laughing and says, "That is what I saw." He then jumps up and puts his robes and cap back on and before the day is done, his illness is completely gone.

The Book of Lieh Tzu describes a gentleman of middle age named Hau Tzu of Yang-li in Sung. He has lost his memory. It is said that if he is given a present in the morning he forgets it by evening; if he is given a present in the evening he forgets it by morning. In the street he forgets to walk and at home he forgets to sit. As the story goes, "today he would not remember yesterday, tomorrow he would not remember today."

His family, understandably upset, invites various healers and diviners to find the cause of his illness, all to no avail. They even call in a doctor, who is just as unable to provide relief for the poor man as anyone. Finally, a Confucian of Lu appears, claiming that he can cure the man. Hau Tzu's family offers him half their property if he succeeds.

The Confucian tells them that this is not a disease which can be divined by the usual methods. He must be cured by having his mind restored and his thoughts changed; then there is a chance that we will recover.

After no doubt impressing the poor forgetful one with his Confucian rhetoric, he begins a curious therapy. He strips Hua Tzu and hides his clothes. Hua Tzu begins looking for them. The Confucian then begins starving Hua Tzu and the patient begins looking for food. He is then shut up in the dark, and begins looking for light.

The Confucian is delighted. He tells Hua Tzu's family, "The sickness is curable. But my arts have been passed down secretly through the generations, and are not disclosed to outsiders. I shall shut out his attendants, and stay alone with him in his room for seven days." They agree and after a long week, the sickness is dispelled.

The only problem is that Hua Tzu wakes up very angry. He dismisses his wife, punishes his sons and chases away the Confucian with a spear! When he is arrested by the authorities and questioned about his strange and violent actions he answers, "Formerly when I forgot, I was boundless; I did not notice whether heaven and earth existed or not. Now suddenly I remember, and all the disasters and recoveries, gains and losses, joys and sorrows, loves and hates of twenty or thirty years past rise up in a thousand tangled threads. I fear that all the disasters, reveries, gains and losses, joys and sorrows, loves and hates still to come will confound my heart just as much. Shall I never again find a moment of forgetfulness?"

The Chinese, as we shall see in the chapter on medicine, attribute consciousness and the seat of the human soul to the heart. It is by softening and opening this seat of understanding and intuition that we may discern those hidden teachers in the world around us. They may appear as fools or madmen or women (though all fools and madmen and women are not enlightened teachers); they may appear as completely nondescript men and women. The jewels they offer us may at first appear to be covered in dust and dung. But with a little elbow grease on our part, we can wipe the filth off and reveal the shining pearl within.

Chapter Sources

Thomas Merton, *The Way of Chuang Tzu*
Clae Waltham, *Chuang Tzu: Genius of the Absurd*
Lin Yutang, *The Wisdom of Laotse*
Gia Fu Feng & Jane English, *Chuang Tsu*
Eva Wong, *Lieh-Tzu, A Taoist Guide to Practical Living*
Victor Mair, *Experimental Essays on Chuang-tzu*
A.C. Graham, *The Book of Lieh Tzu*
John Blofeld, *Gateway to Wisdom*

7

To Dream the Impossible Dream

There was once a rich man from the country of Ch'ou. He had a huge estate and many workers, whom he drove unmercifully. Day after day they toiled under the hot sun to fill the coffers of the rich man.

One of these was an old man who had been working for the rich man's family for many years. His body was nearly worn out with hard work and little rest; his muscles were stringy and his breath came in gasps, but still the foreman drove him on. At the end of the day, however, once he had laid his weary head down on his rice bag pillow, he dreamed he was a rich man with a huge estate. All night long he was waited upon by servants, fed rare delicacies and entertained by beautiful women who played lovely and haunting melodies and danced ancient and graceful dances for him. He spent the entire dream in idle pursuit and as a finale he dandled his fat young sons on his knees and laughed into the night.

Of course, upon waking, the old man was once again the lowly laborer who spent his day in endless toil. When the noonday break came and he sat heavily down to eat his rice, his face showed his weariness. His friends would then try to console him. "No need," he would say. "By day I am a slave to the rich man but at night I *am* the rich man. I spend half my life working his fields but the other half I spend in ease and comfort. Therefore do not pity me."

On the other hand, when the rich man, who spent his days in useless frivolity, laid his head upon his silken pillow, he tossed and turned and groaned all through the night. He dreamed he was a common laborer in his fields. All through the dream he worked, bent over, with muscles aching and sweat pouring down his face. For his noon meal he ate the coarsest rice with no flavor and, instead of sweet wine, he drank brackish water, not even tea. At the end of his labors he collapsed on his pallet, all alone in his little hut—his wife had died long ago and his children had left to find a better master far away. His life meant unending toil, with no rest and no respite, for his master was cruel and demanding. This life was truly miserable.

When he awoke in the morning the rich man's muscles ached as if he truly had worked in the fields all night, his bed was soaked with sweat and his mouth tasted dry and dusty.

When he complained to his friends they told him, "Don't worry. By night you may suffer but by day you are a rich man, well respected in the business community, and you have far more than you will ever need. You are at the top of the ladder; that is why you dream at night that you are at the bottom. You cannot have it both ways. Things must balance. That is why you have those vexing dreams."

The rich man thought about this, as each day he awakened more weary than the day before. He took to walking over his estate to try to relax his agitated mind. He saw his workers there, toiling in the hot sun all day. He noticed in particular one old man who never stopped working; he was shriveled and bent over by many years of hard labor. Yet he never complained, never shirked, and always had a small smile on his face. "I envy that man," he thought. "He has nothing yet seems so much happier than me."

The old worker saw the rich man watching him. He noticed how the rich man looked drawn and tired. His skin was pasty and drooped from his face in an unhealthy way. He noticed that the hands of the rich man, as soft and manicured as they were, shook and that his soft, fat body looked weak and tremulous.

After a time, the rich man decided it would be better if he changed his ways, since he was not happy with the way things were going. He lightened up on his workers, gave them more time off and began himself to be more physical, which, after a time, made him feel immeasurably better. Not only that, but his nightmares went away and he slept more soundly than he had in years.

As for the old man, he too began to enjoy his waking life more and did not need to escape each night into dreams. Instead he too slept soundly. As the ancient sage says: "The True Men of old forgot themselves when awake and did not dream when they slept."

8

The Slippery Art of Wu Wei

*The true character of wu wei is not mere inactivity but perfect action —
because it is act without activity.*
Thomas Merton

*It succeeds by being rather than doing, by attitude rather than act, by
attraction rather than compulsion.*
Holmes Welch

*One whose mind is a mirror of his situation, unaware of himself and
therefore making no distinction between advantage and danger, will act with
absolute assurance, and nothing will stand in his way.*
A.C. Graham

*He who practices the Way does less and less every day, does less and goes
on doing less until he reaches the point where he does nothing, does nothing
yet there is nothing that is not done!*
Chuang Tzu

Wu wei is one of the most difficult concepts in Taoist philosophy.
Roughly translated, it means "doing nothing." Westerners who are first
introduced to Taoism sometimes think the term wu wei means sitting
around and doing nothing—a passive acceptance of life and a sort of
mushy, hopeless attitude. Nothing could be further from the truth. Alan
Watts calls wu wei " a form of intelligence—that is, of knowing the
principles, structures, and trends of human and natural affairs so well
that one uses the least amount of energy in dealing with them" or "the
innate wisdom of the nervous system." Far from being a passive ac-

ceptance or resignation to things, it is instead an active and dynamic engagement with things as they are. It is a way of working with the dynamics of any situation in order to find the path of least resistance and then following through.

The true meaning of the phrase wu wei is something like "not doing anything that is not natural" or "not doing anything that does not have its roots in Tao." Joseph Needham explains it like this:

[Wu wei means] "refraining from activity contrary to Nature"; i.e., from insisting on going against the grain of things, from trying to make materials perform functions for which they are unsuitable, from exerting force in the human affairs when the man of insight could see that it would be doomed to failure, and that subtle methods of persuasion, of simply letting things alone to take their own course, would bring about the desired result.

Wu wei is the opposite of *yu wei* or action with useless effort. It is coupled with spontaneity and a deep awareness of what is happening in any situation, allowing one to discern whether it would be better to act or not to act (which, of course, is what Hamlet was *really* talking about). It is a kind of spontaneity which, as Clae Waltham says, cannot be captured, only fostered. It is a kind of perception of the currents of any situation and our place in it. Lao Tzu says that:

Teaching without words and working without doing,
Are understood by very few.
          (Chapter 43)

And:

Do you think you can take over the universe and improve it?
I do not believe it can be done.
The universe is sacred.
You cannot improve it.
If you try to change it, you will ruin it.
If you try to hold it, you will lose it.
          (Chapter 29)

Trying to hold tight to any situation, trying to figure out just what exactly is going on, and most of all, trying to control the situation through force of will or use of "knowledge" or intellectual gymnastics is foolish and will in all probability land us on our faces in the mud. Chuang Tzu said:

The knowledge of the ancients was perfect. How perfect? At first, they did not know that there were things. This is the most perfect knowledge; nothing can be added. Next, they knew there were things, but did not yet make distinctions between them. Next, they made distinction between them, but they did not yet pass judgements upon them. When judgements were passed, Tao was destroyed.

Taoists are lovers of simplicity and naturalness. Chuang Tzu said the wisdom of the ancients was perfect because they did not know there were things—they did not differentiate, they did not catalogue, they did not separate one thing from another, one state of mind from another, one state of being from another. In this way they were able to remain pure and close to the original undifferentiated Tao.

My tai ji teacher, David Cheng, was fond of telling us it is our mind that gets us into trouble. It is our mind, our discriminating intellect that creates all sorts of problems for us, then thinks it can figure a way out of them. But then again, David said, without our mind we would not know how to drive a car or take a bus or make our way to tai ji class! We would not understand what language he was speaking or how to follow his movements. Our mind is a tool, he said—a wonderful, useful tool. Sometimes, for example, we need to discriminate; we need to be able to look at a situation dispassionately and intelligently and see if it is a situation or a relationship or a job or a person that is good for us or bad for us. This is a good way to use that marvelous tool, the mind. But let's put it back in the toolbox when we're done with it. Let's not leave it lying around where we can step on it or trip over it all the time.

How are we to learn to work with this slippery concept, wu wei? The old maxim, "learn by doing" applies here as well as anywhere else. It is a matter of going slowly, the slower the better. The wonderful dance of tai ji is a perfect example of wu wei in action. The gentle movements are done as slowly as possible, so that it becomes a sort of dancing meditation.

Often we find ourselves in trouble simply because we are going too fast, disregarding signs of trouble that we would have seen if only we had been going a little slower. All too often we get caught up in the rush; our whole culture is based on it. Get ahead! Do it now! So stop to listen quietly to the voices within—the still, small voices as well as the loud and clear ones. It's hard, if not downright impossible, to hear them when we are going fast, listening instead to the constant blare of the world around us. Sometimes the right thing to do is not to do anything.

Wu wei is an attitude, an approach to life itself. When we become sensitive to the current of change all around us we will be able to make intelligent decisions at all times, using the innate wisdom of our bodies and energy systems as well as our minds. As A.C. Graham, in his wonderful translation of the *Book of Lieh Tzu*, says, "Nowhere is there a principle which is right in all circumstances, or an action that is wrong in all circumstances."

Wu wei is learning how to conserve our energy and not spend it frivolously or in fear or confusion. Sometimes it is far easier and actually in our best interest and in the best interest of the actual situation to do nothing or to find some way around the situation rather than trying to go through it. Blofeld tells us that "a Taoist conserves his energy by easily according with and adapting himself to each situation."

We may be sick or injured and lying in bed, trying hard to figure out what is going on, why this is happening to us and when will it be over? While the body, mind and spirit are tied up in knots trying to decipher this maddening puzzle, we are getting nowhere, slowly. How much easier, though it takes a little practice, to just let go and let be what is and learn how to be okay while we're not feeling okay. Sometimes there just isn't anything to do, and the best course is to relax and and do nothing. Later on the situation may change and there will be something that we *can* do to help ourselves. Then, with the same grace that we did nothing, we can do something.

Oftentimes doing something is not better, more important or even more helpful than doing nothing. When we feel stuck and unable to move, what we are actually doing is storing energy to be able to make a move, or the kind of move that will actually mean something. Like water, our energy must slowly collect before it can spill over the dam. Often when we think we'll never get out of a rut or never be able to move again, being patient and conserving our energy will help us make an even greater move when the time is right.

By learning to relax and discover the intrinsic flow of events that contain and are contained by our lives we can reach some measure of security and perhaps even wisdom. Chuang Tzu likens this state to that of a drunken man:

> A drunken man falls out of a cart; though he may suffer, he does not die. His bones are the same as other people's; but he meets the accident in a different way. His spirit is the condition of security. He is not conscious of riding in the cart; neither is he conscious of falling out of it. Ideas of life, death and fear cannot penetrate his breast; and so he does not suffer from contact with objective circumstances. And if such security is to be got from wine, how much more is to be gotten from spontaneity.

In this passage, Chuang Tzu describes wu wei as spontaneity, a total indentification with the present moment. For in reality there is no other moment than the one we are in. Alan Watts says, "you can think about the past and you can think about the future, but since you do that thinking now, the present is inescapable." So then how to develop this sense of spontaneity, this sensitivity to the here and now? A.C. Graham says:

If he wishes to return to the Way he must discard knowledge, cease to make distinctions, refuse to impose his will and his principles on nature, recover the spontaneity of the newborn child, allow his actions to be 'so of themselves' *like physical processes.* (Author's italics).

Another way is to follow the advice of John Blofeld:

Caring not for what people may think of him, he takes no pride in heroics, for its own sake, so he looks for the easiest way round. That is not to say that he willingly surrenders an objective, only that he will not attempt the impossible, nor expend more energy than is strictly necessary to attain the possible. By no means lazy, he conserves his powers in order to make the most of them.

Chapter Sources

Thomas Merton, *The Way of Chuang Tzu*
Holmes Welch, *Taoism: The Parting of the Way*
A.C. Graham, *The Book of Lieh Tzu*
Clae Waltham, *Chuang Tzu: Genius of the Absurd*
Joseph Needham, *Science and Civilization in China*
Gia Fu Feng & Jane English, *Tao Te Ching*
John Blofeld, *Taoism, the Road to Immortality*

9

The Uncarved Block

The principles treasured by the Taoist are simplicity, equilibrium, harmony and quietude.
Hua-Ching Ni

Their ideal was the undifferentiated 'natural' condition of life, before the institution of private property, before the appearance of pro-feudalism with its lords and 'high kings,' its priests, artisans and augurs, at the beginning of the Bronze Age.
Joseph Needham

"Rabbit's very clever," said Pooh thoughtfully. "Yes," said Piglet, "Rabbit's clever." "And he has a brain." "Yes," said Piglet, "Rabbit has a brain." There was a long silence. "I suppose," said Pooh, "that's why he never understands anything."
Winnie the Pooh

The principle of the Uncarved Block or *P'u* in Chinese is an essential element of Taoist philosophy and practice. It is the concept of the simple, uncluttered and natural man and woman and their way of life. This way of being in the world is in perfect accord, of course, with the teachings of Lao Tzu and Chuang Tzu.

Fame or self: Which matters more?
Self or wealth: Which is more precious?
Gain or loss: Which is more painful?

He who is attached to things will suffer much.

He who saves will suffer heavy loss.
He who knows when to stop does not find himself in trouble.
He will stay forever safe.
(Chapter 44)

The ancient Taoists were not only content to live simple, natural lives but actually felt there was a solid advantage to doing so. It isn't necessary to "drop out" and live in the mountains away from the world in order to live a simple, natural life. What we're actually talking about is an *internal* state of simplicity and naturalness. We may be involved in all kinds of things, from running a large clinic to teaching a group of children or overseeing a complicated business. Yet all of this need not stop us from having internal simplicity and naturalness.

It is when we allow outside pressures and complications to take up residence within us that we run into trouble and lose our sense of safety and spontaneity, which to Taoists is very serious indeed. How often do we meet someone at a party or other gathering and are asked by way of introduction, "So what is it that you do?", as if a description of our work life defines us. Why aren't we asked or why don't we ask, "What is it that interests you in life? What turns you on?" That information would probably go much further in describing or defining us to others and to ourselves.

Remember the principle of wu wei? It is often in *not doing* that we get the most done! Often *not doing* defines who we are much more thoroughly than all the *doing* we could possible produce. Yet we get caught up in an urge to produce to some extent. After all, if I were following the principle of *wu wei* exactly, I wouldn't even be writing this book!

It is said that the Tao will manifest itself to everyone, sooner or later. There is no rush or even set time when this will or should happen. But all the teachers, both ancient and modern, stress that it is in the natural simplicity of our being that we can best manifest and embrace the Tao. The question is, how do we do this?

Hua-Ching Ni says: "A natural human being is directed by his spiritual energy and causes appropriate responses not by his need, but by his pure spontaneity." Remember, spontaneity is something that rises from deep within our true nature and cannot be artificially produced. This spontaneity also has something of the "holy fool" in it. Max Kaltnemark says the true Taoist must, in his perfect simplicity, have the appearance of a fool.

Indeed, there is a vast tradition of "holy fools" throughout the world. Here, however, we will limit ourselves to the Taoist version of this interesting and amusing figure.

N. J. Girardot describes him thusly:

> Taoist images of madness are related to the mystical experience of the chaos condition and to the unique effortless freedom of wu wei, the sage's playful freedom beyond human, or even humane, bounds. The Taoist as a 'demented drifter' is aloof and indifferent to the normal order of the world. From the perspective of his belly knowledge, the Taoist is a wayfarer who knows that 'the way things appear to be—permanent, predictable, manageable—is not the way things really are in an ultimate vision of the real.'

The "holy fool" is one who is not actually a fool in the real sense, but is called that by a society which does not understand his or her actions. This is because the Taoist is operating outside of the norm, or what society at large considers normal. To the highly rigid and structured Confucian society of the Han dynasty and beyond, the Taoists, with their free and "wild" (in the sense of natural) ways, were often regarded as fools and rebellious outcasts, content to live "in the world but not of it."

And, because they were basing their understanding and approach to life on something other than the status quo, they were considered rebels and malcontents or just empty-headed dreamers. It was a state not always comfortable for them either, as Lao Tzu puts it so poignantly:

> Is there a difference between yes and no?
> Is there a difference between good and evil?
> Must I fear what others fear? What nonsense!
> Other people are contented, enjoying the sacrificial feast of the ox.
> In spring some go to the park, and climb the terrace.
>
> But I alone am drifting, not knowing where I am.
> Like a new born babe before it learns how to smile,
> I am alone, without a place to go.
>
> Others have more than they need, but I alone have nothing.
> I am a fool. Oh, yes! I am confused.
> Other men are clear and bright.
> But I alone am dim and weak.
> Other men are sharp and clever.
> But I alone am dull and stupid.
> Oh, I drift like the waves of the sea,
> Without direction, like a restless wind.
>
> Everyone is busy,
> But I alone am aimless and depressed.
> I am different.
> I am nourished by the great mother.
> (Chapter 20)

This is a beautiful way to describe the often sad feeling of being different or cut off from the crowd. Taoists have to get used to going their own way and being misunderstood, or even ridiculed because of their beliefs and way of life. But isn't it better to be called a fool than to actually be one? After all, isn't the unhealthy, unbalanced and unconscious way that most people live true foolishness?

When we first become aware and sensitive to the subtle currents of energy in our being—spiritual, physical and emotional—it can be painful. Many of us are not used to being particularly sensitive and we sometimes come up hard against our limitations, created both by the world and by ourselves. We may feel alienated and cut off from those around us who are busy rushing after the next thrill, the next high, the next desperate way of trying to be real.

While there are, even today, many students and followers of the Way, they are often hard to identify. You may see a wide eyed, open-ended look that is offered when you least expect it, or perhaps a certain loose limbed way of walking, a sign of one who is attuned to his or her own energy flow. You may encounter an attitude toward healing or an openness to the use of herbs or acupuncture, or a way of unaffected talking, and a deep awareness of the importance of good listening. Or else you may hear a good strong laugh, coming from deep in the belly, a laugh that says yes, I am a believer in the sanctity and miraculous unfolding of each precious moment in the Tao and I am willing to share that feeling, that awareness, that experience with you.

There is also the shared knowledge that most of what passes for "reality" in the collective unconscious is actually a huge joke, a play, a pantomime. This is different from the Hindu sense of the world as an illusion, or the Christian/Judaic idea of life as a vale of tears or some sort of proving ground for what comes after death.

To the Taoists, what we experience on the material plane is as real as the nose on our face. Yet at the same time it is also a bit of a dream. Chuang Tzu once dreamed that he was a butterfly, flitting merrily about the multi-colored flowers. When he awoke he exclaimed, "How is it that I can be sure that instead of Chuang Tzu dreaming that I am a butterfly, I am not a butterfly dreaming that I am Chuang Tzu?"

In another place he says:

Men in general bustle about and toil; the sage seems unlettered and without "knowledge."...When people dream they do not know that they are dreaming. In their dream they may even interpret dreams. Only when they awake they begin to know that they dreamed. By and by comes the greater awakening, and then we shall find out that life itself is a great dream. All the while the fools think they are awake, and that they have knowledge. Making nice discriminations, they differentiate between princes and grooms. How stupid!

The experience of "life as a dream" frees us from the awful burden of always having to do it right, of toiling under the enormous weight of having to be 'on the job' at all times. It frees us also to make mistakes and allows us the freedom, the privilege, of starting over again, time after time if need be. And, most of all, it frees us to change, to begin anew, to metamorphosize into whatever lovely and colorful butterfly we always wanted to be but never felt the permission or strength to become.

Remember, the Tao does not judge, it does not punish, it does not condemn. We do that ourselves. And as we judge, so also can we forgive ourselves and others who have wronged us through their own mistaken sense of reality. And we find, in that forgiveness, an even greater sense of freedom and unlimited potential—for growth, exploration, and an enlarged sense of the Tao and our place in it.

Through forgiveness, through trust, through taking chances with ourselves and others, and through returning to our "original nature"— our own sweet simple and natural self, our own "uncarved block"— that we can begin the journey that leads back to its beginning, to our original nature, or Tao.

Once, after a particularly poignant lesson by his teacher, Lieh Tzu decided that, in truth, he had never learned anything, so he went home and for three years did not leave his house.

> He cooked meals for his wife,
> Served food to his pigs as though they were human,
> Treated all things as equally as his kin,
> From carved jade he returned to the unhewn block,
> Till his single shape stood forth, detached from all things.
> He was free of tangles
> Once and for all, to the end of his life.

Or, as Hua-Ching Ni puts it:

Become the kind of person whose wish is infectious. Then what you want, others will want, and while you seem to do nothing (wu wei), everything will be done. The power of the infectious wish comes from certain virtues: compassion, moderation, and humility. These virtues and their power are te.

Te cannot be achieved, however, until you have erased the aggressive patterns etched by society into your nature. You must return to your natural self, to p'u. You must discard morality and ambition, for if you keep these you will never be capable of compassion, moderation and humility. When you discard some of your wishes, you will have them all.

Chapter Sources

Hua-Ching Ni, *Tao: The Subtle Universal Law
    and the Integral Way of Life*
Joseph Needham, *Science and Civilization in China*
A.A. Milne, *Winnie the Pooh*
Gia-Fu Feng & Jane English, *Tao Te Ching*
Max Kaltnemark, *Lao Tzu and Taoism*
 N.J. Girardot, *Myth and Meaning in Early Taoism*
Clae Waltham, *Chuang Tzu: Genius of the Absurd*
A.C. Graham, *The Book of Lieh Tzu*

10

The Watercourse Way

The fluidity of water is not the result of any effort on the part of the water, but is its natural property.
Chuang Tzu

Under heaven nothing is more soft and yielding than water.
Yet for attacking the solid and strong, nothing is better;
It has no equal.
The weak can overcome the strong;
The supple can overcome the stiff.
Under Heaven everyone knows this,
Yet no one puts it into practice.
(Chapter 78)

The image of water is used over and over again in Taoism to de-note the qualities of humbleness, flexibility, adaptability, persistence and acceptance. Indeed, the Tao itself is likened to water by Lao Tzu:

The highest good is like water.
Water gives life to the ten thousand things and does not strive.
It flows in places men reject and so is like the Tao.
(Chapter 8)

This is both a description of the humbleness which Taoists felt proper of the sage as well as a dig to the Confucians and their idea of the proper gentleman who never got his hands dirty.

Alan Watts calls Taoism itself the Watercourse Way, citing numer-ous references to water throughout the *Tao Te Ching* as well as in Chuang

Tzu. He also quotes from the *Kuan Tzu*, a book from the late 4th century BCE :

> Water is the blood of the earth, and flows through its muscles and veins. Therefore it is said that water is something that has complete faculties...It is accumulated in Heaven and earth, and stored up in the various things (of the world). It comes forth in metal and stone, and is concentrated in living creatures. Therefore it is said that water is something special.

The passage ends by saying:

> Hence the solution for the sage who would transform the world lies in water. Therefore when water is uncontaminated, men's hearts are upright. When water is pure, the people's hearts are at ease. Men's hearts being upright, their desires do not become dissolute. The people's hearts being upright, their conduct is without evil. Hence the Sage, when he rules the world, does not teach men one by one, or house by house, but takes water as his key.

Water takes whatever shape it finds itself in and is the embodiment of patience and perseverance, able to cut through mountains drop by drop. Elsewhere, Lao Tzu describes the Sage-Ruler:

> Why is the sea king of a hundred streams?
> Because it lies below them,
> Therefore it is the king of a hundred streams.
> If the sage would guide the people, he must serve with
>   humility.
> If he would lead them, he must follow behind.
> In this way when the sage rules, the people will not feel
>   oppressed.
> When he stands before them, they will not be harmed.
> The whole world will support him and will not tire of him.
> Because he does not compete,
> He does not meet competition.
>   (Chapter 66)

Humbleness means having the ability to follow behind instead of leading the band, of ruling a people as well as one's self in a way that least resembles leadership, the wu wei form of governing.

"Tao in the world," says Lao Tzu, "is like a river flowing home to the sea."

Again and again, Taoism uses the image of water to emphasize the soft overcoming the hard. Water can overcome obstacles, not only by going around them but by simply biding its time and slowly eroding the obstacle, bit by tiny bit, until eventually a canyon is formed! This is a central tenant of Taoist philosophy. We can meet obstacles in our lives and find ways to creatively and constructively deal with them. The idea is not to avoid or run away from them or, on the other hand, try to ram head on into them, but by going slowly and assuming the quality of water, we can, perhaps, find a way to either flow around, over or under them. Like water, be patient and persevere enough to realize that in time things will change, because that is the nature of all things. *The only constant is change.*

Water does not judge. Water does not discriminate, it does not attach labels or attempt to use its will to bend objects or situations to its own specifications. We all want to shape situations to our own specifications in order to be happy. We all want things to go right for us as much as possible; we all want to be in the driver's seat. But as Graham says: "The alternation of joy and sorrow, life and death, *is itself the Way,* and we run counter to it when we strive to perpetuate joy and life." (author's italics). Later on he says, "We must respond differently to different situations; action should depend, not only on subjective standards, but on the objective situation, to which we should adjust ourselves with the immediacy of the shadow adjusting itself to the moving body."

Hua-Ching Ni wrote this beautiful passage in his book *The Gentle Path of Spiritual Progress:*

People have different natural cycles which can be organized according to the five different phases of energy. Sometimes you do better in life and other times you do poorly. When your cycle is high, you enjoy your life more than when you are having difficulties in a low cycle. To harmonize the flow of your life, don't become excited by the high points or depressed by the low. *Always remember the high is built by the low.* You should respect the times when you are in a low cycle, the times when you are a nobody. Don't struggle to be a somebody, because you will only be a somebody when other people say you are somebody. "Somebody" is built on the moments when you are a nobody. This guidance is not the same as ordinary teachings that only look for high respect and exaltation and don't value the low. When you look up to the high, spiritually and emotionally you are low. When you respect the low, spiritually and emotionally you are high.

When people have a low cycle, they think of it in an emotional way and feel terrible. They want to die or kill themselves. They feel boring, unattractive and uninteresting. They receive no attention or respect from anyone, and they don't love themselves either. *They don't realize that their low cycle can make them wise.* Life is built up by each uninteresting moment, not just by excitement. (author's italics).

To the Taoist, exalting the high in place of the low is to lose sight of the truth of how things really are. Our lives are filled with endless moments when nothing seems to be happening, when we seem to be stuck in a rut or are making no progress at all. But according to the Taoists, it is in these moments, these dull and uninteresting moments, that we can be building the foundation to sagehood. Becoming a sage, or an emotionally and spiritually balanced person, is not all fun and games! As Master Ni says, life is built up by each uninteresting moment. But if we can take on the attributes of water and develop our sense of flexibility and patience, we can become like the old man whom Chuang Tzu describes who fell two hundred and forty feet down a cataract and emerged downstream unharmed.

It seems that Confucius (who figures in many of Chuang Tzu's stories) was looking down into the gorge at Lu where a great waterfall crashed down to a huge roiling chasm so violent that no fish, tortoises or even alligators could survive there. Suddenly he notices an old man appear to tumble over the falls into the maelstrom. Horrified, Confucius, along with several of his disciples, runs downstream in hope of saving the poor unfortunate, only to find him strolling merrily along the bank, singing to himself!

Cautiously, Confucius approaches the man and says to him, "I thought perhaps you were some sort of spirit, but now I see that you are indeed flesh and blood. But tell me, how did you manage to survive that plunge into the river?"

"Oh that," answers the man. "That is simple. I merely enter the water at the center of its whirl. I let myself flow along with it, not trying to impose my will upon it, then leave it when it whirls the opposite way. It is all completely natural to me and my success is sure."

"What can you mean by this?" asked Confucius. "How is it natural to you and how can you be so sure of success?"

"Well," answers the man, before he again wanders off, "I grew up on dry land and so am at home on it. At the same time, I also grew up by the river and so am at home in the water. I don't really know how it is I do these things—I just do them. Therefore my success is assured."

Chapter Sources

Alan Watts, *Tao: The Watercourse Way*
Gia-Fu Feng & Jane English, *Tao Te Ching*
Hua-Ching Ni, *The Gentle Path of Spiritual Progress*
A.C. Graham, *The Book of Lieh Tzu*

II

The Eternal Dance of Yin and Yang

*Yin/Yang is the Way of heaven and earth,
the fundamental principle of the myriad things,
the father and mother of change and transformation,
the root of conception and destruction.*
Su-wen

*The single most important point to remember about polarity is that yin
and yang energies are not separate energies; they are one and the same energy,
but with two different charges.*
Mantak Chia

The principle of *yin* and *yang* is fundamental to any understanding of Taoist philosophy, sexual yoga and what we know of today as Chinese medicine. Indeed, it is the principle of how the very universe came into being and how it continues to manifest itself. Lao Tzu says:

The Tao begot one.
One begot two.
Two begot three.
And three begot the ten thousand things.
The ten thousand things carry yin and embrace yang.
They achieve harmony by combining these forces.
(Chapter 42)

The one is the beginning of being, which has its source in non-being or Tao. The two is, of course, yin and yang. The three is the three

treasures, which we will discuss in chapters on medicine and meditation. It can also be thought of as the three levels of existance—spiritual, physical, and mental, which we all contain within ourselves. The
ten thousand things are the material manifestations, or simply, the material world.

To the Chinese, the universe is divided into polarities—yin and
yang. In this way, all elements are paired and balanced with each other.
These elements consist of primal qualities: male and female, night and
day, sun and moon, moist and dry, dark and light, fire and water. It is
through awareness and experience of this interdependence and inter-
relationship that the universe, and we humans within it, remain in balance.

Originally yang stood for the bright side of the hill, the side facing
the sun. Yin stood for the shady side, away from the sun. The ancient
Taoists, those natural philosophers of balance and change, used the
concepts of yin and yang to symbolize the polarity of existence. Everything that exists can be assigned either to yin or yang, thus identifying
its polar aspect.

The qualities of yin are darkness, water, cold, rest, inward and
downward direction, stillness, receptivity and what we think of as fe-
maleness. The qualities of yang are brightness, heat, activity, upward
and outward direction, aggressiveness, expansion and what we think
of as maleness.

The yin/yang theory does not merely set opposites against each
other. The well known tai ji symbol, one of the oldest symbols known
to humankind and certainly one of the most powerful, shows the two
primal forces of the universe, each enfolded within the other. You'll
also notice that each contains a piece of the other. Just as all males have
a female aspect, so do all females have a certain maleness (Jung's anima
and animus). There is no light which does not contain an element of
darkness, and there is no darkness without its tinge of light.

Yin and yang complement each other. That is, rather than oppos-
ing each other in primal struggle, they create each other, control each
other, and even transform into each other. Alan Watts likens them to
lovers wrestling rather than enemies fighting.

Manfred Porkert, in his book on Chinese medicine says:

Changes of every kind—from the transitory changes of state to deep-rooted
fundamental transformation—are brought about by the active principle, yang,
but it is the constructive principle, yin, that causes everything to assume a
stable, concrete form (or cease to exist altogether).

Hua-Ching Ni compares it to the tendency of electrons to propel themselves away from the nucleus of the atom which is balanced by the force of the protons to attract the electrons to the center, without which the atom would disintegrate.

The principle of yin and yang suggests the inherent movement of the Tao. After all, life implies movement. In order to retain the flexibility that Lao Tzu talks about, we have to sustain the quality of *movement* in our lives. This doesn't mean running around madly from one scene to another, one relationship to another, one religion to another, but rather something internal, an openness to change and to new experience. It implies a dynamic *engagement* with life. The principle of wu wei does not mean passive acceptance in the mushy, fatalistic sense; it refers to a *willful* acceptance of the way things are and an openness to the ability and likelihood that they will change and so will we change too.

We all have both yin and yang qualities within ourselves. The balance of these two qualities is not static and concrete, but moving and shifting. At times our yin side asserts itself, at other times our yang. No one aspect is right for every situation; it is best to recognize and be willing to work with the ever shifting balance of power in any situation or moment.

Innate instincts belong to yin while acquired skills belong to yang. Without the polarity of these two primal qualities the universe itself would stagnate and possibly deconstruct. In the world of reality as we know it, or the realm of the ten thousand things, yin and yang help define each other and in doing so help us discriminate one thing or quality from another.

Lao Tzu says:

Under heaven all can see beauty as beauty only because there
     is ugliness.
All can know good as good only because there is evil.

Therefore having and not having arise together.
Difficult and easy compliment each other.
Long and short contrast each other;
High and low rest upon each other;
Voice and sound harmonize each other;
Front and back follow one another.
          (Chapter 2)

By way of contrasts, we are able to differentiate one thing from another. To the Taoists, nothing exists of itself; all things exist *in relation* to something else. Even we ourselves, as independent and isolated as we often feel, exist only in relation to all other life forms on the planet.

Viewed in this light, we can find solace and strength in the interpenetration and interdependence of all life. No man is an island indeed.

This vision of unity and joyful diversity can empower us to live a life of harmonious and exciting engagement. By being aware and sensitive to the balance and subtle shifts of our own yin/yang qualities we are better able to make proper decisions and conduct ourselves with greater integrity and foresight in our dealings with others. As Ellen M. Chen says:

The opposites have a vital need for each other, just as no human being can live fully without relationships. . .to attempt to do so is either to stagnate or to court mental and spiritual malaise. This interaction of the opposites has its naive, elementary stage in unconscious reaction, a force impelled by nature but not yet acting consciously as an integrated individual and therefore giving rise to conflict in the two sides of man's nature as well as the conflict between the needs of the individual and society. It is for the individual to find the balance and this requires spontaneous adaptation and adjustment to every situation and relationship in life. It is attained by seeing the extremes, the opposites, and understanding their significance. As everything in the manifest world, the realm of dualism arises from the relationship between the two polar opposites, the *yin* and the *yang*, it is the main concern of life to understand them and keep them in balance and harmony.

Chapter Sources

Ilza Veith, *The Yellow Emperor's Classic of Internal Medicine*
R.H. Van Gulik, *Sexual Life in Ancient China*
Alan Watts, *The Watercourse Way*
Mantak Chia, *Taoist Secrets of Love: Cultivating Male Sexual Energy*
Manfred Porkert with Christian Ullmann, *Chinese Medicine*
Hua-Ching Ni, *Tao: The Subtle Universal Law and the
    Integral Way of Life*
Gia Fu Feng & Jane English, *Tao Te Ching*
Ellen Chen, *Tao Te Ching*
Daniel Reid, *The Tao of Health, Sex & Longevity*
J.C. Cooper, *Taoism, the Way of the Mystic*

12

The Tao of Sex and Relationship

As far as Taoists are concerned, the only important distinctions regarding sexual activities are those between healthy and unhealthy habits.
Daniel P. Reid

Like the breath of life, sex is vital to the continuation of human beings. As a natural euphoriant, sex is vital to humanity's mental well-being. Unknown to most people, sex is vital to mankind's spiritual elevation.
Stephen T. Chang

Refining one's awareness of sexual energy — with or without a partner — is one of the simplest ways of humans to return to pure consciousness and experience the deepest rhythms of life.
Mantak Chia

The ancient Taoist view of sex is extremely different from modern attitudes about this most primal of human expressions. It teaches us how to use this primal urge to facilitate greater communication and trust levels with our partners, including aspects of health (physical, emotional and psychological), and spirituality. It is different from other tantric paths, such as those found in the Hindu tradition, in that it is simpler, easier to learn and use, and not as concerned with elaborate ritual and visualization techniques. Instead, it is concerned with the basic male/female attraction and interaction as well as the ability to use our own individual sexual energy to further ourselves in our quest for better health and a greater sense of spirituality.

As Van Gulik describes it in his seminal work, *Sexual Life in Ancient China:*

...the ancient Chinese attitude to sex, namely an unreserved, joyful acception of all the varied aspects of human procreation, ranging from the smallest biological details of carnal congress to the most elevated spiritual love of which that congress is the seal and confirmation.

Viewed as the human counterpart of the cosmic creative process, sexual intercourse was looked upon with reverence, and never associated with moral guilt or sin. The cosmic prototype hallowed the flesh, never considered an abomination. No difference was felt between, for instance, the rain sprinkling the fields, and the semen fecundating the womb; or between the rich, wet soil ready for the seed, and moist vagina of the woman prepared for sexual congress.

As with Taoist philosophy itself, Taoist sexual yoga is governed by cycles and seasons, by an awareness of our own energetic system as well as that of our partner. Its attitudes and practices are ways to tap into that energy and not only share it with our partner but direct it within ourselves. It casts no moral judgments upon the sexual act itself and would laugh good naturedly at anyone who tried to do so. Instead, it offers healthy and productive ways of being sexual, both within our bodies and with those whom we love.

The Art of the Bedchamber

...if one partakes of all the various magic drugs and nurtures one's three natures, while at the same time being ignorant of the Art of the Bedchamber, those drugs and disciplines will prove to be without effect.
Ko Hung

The true joy of loving is an ecstasy of two bodies and souls mingling and uniting in poetry. Once a man has found an ideal partner he must try and make love to her ecstatically and poetically.
Jolan Chang

The Art of the Bedchamber was orginated by Huang Ti, the Yellow Emperor himself, that ancient, perhaps mythical sage-king the Chinese are so fond of. The teachings themselves are believed to have been handed down by three immortal maidens who came to him one evening when he was burdened by the heavy weight of royal responsibility to his concubines. Because he was the symbol of the health and welfare of the entire kingdom, his ability to cohabit with his vast assemblage of concubines and wives was a symbol of the vitality of the kingdom as a whole. And so, with literally hundreds and sometimes thousands of women to satisfy, it is no wonder that the Son of Heaven found himself becoming extremely worn out! Fortunately for him, and fortunately for the men of today, there is a way to not only satisfy both his partner and himself, but also to retain his vital energy in the process. This is what the three immortal maidens taught Huang Ti so long ago.

As Jolan Chang describes the scene, the emperor is distraught and overwhelmed by his divine duties. "I am weary and in disharmony," Huang Ti is said to have told his illustrious visitors. "I am sad and apprehensive. What shall I do about this?"

He is told by Su Nu or the Plain Girl that all sickness of man can be attributed to faulty ways of loving. Women are stronger in sex and constitution and those who do not know the Tao of Loving will die before their time, without enjoying the pleasure of living.

At first Huang Ti is not convinced. Those long nights with his multiple wives have been wearing him out! "I do not think I want to make love anymore," he answers. "What do you think of that?"

"No, you must not do that," is the reply. He is then told how yin and yang have their activities and changes and that humans must not do anything against the course of nature (wu wei).

"When yin and yang are not in communication they can no longer compensate and harmonize each other," he is told. He is then told that making love and knowing how to control one's emission is called "the return of the jing," which is very beneficial to man's health. At this the Emperor perked up and spent the next several nights in close communion with his three immortal teachers and thus the Art of the Bedroom was born.

Van Gulik quotes an excerpt from a former Han bibliography describing this Art of the Bedroom, or *fang-chung*, as follows:

The Art of the Bedchamber constitutes the climax of human emotions, it encompasses the Supreme Way (Tao). Therefore the Saintly Kings of antiquity regulated man's outer pleasures in order to restrain his inner passions and made detailed rules of sexual intercourse. An old record says: "The ancients created sexual pleasure thereby to regulate all human affairs." If one regulates his sexual pleasure he will feel at peace and attain a high age. If, on the other hand, one abandons himself to its pleasure disregarding the rules set forth in the abovementioned treatises one will fall ill and harm one's very life.

What exactly is this mysterious art? Actually, it's very simple. And, as with all Taoist practices, it involves balance, harmony and naturalness. It also involves surrender, trust and self-discipline (as opposed to self-denial). At the very heart of the Art of the Bedroom or the Tao of Sex is the notion that woman is both energetically and sexually superior to man.

Woman is considered to be the repository of inexhaustible yin while the man is caught up in his all too quickly exhaustible yang. Applying this belief to other aspects of life, it also means women are more often capable of sustained efforts and are more conscious of long term goals and effects. And men, unconsciously acknowledging the superiority of women in this way, have feared and envied them and, consciously and unconsciously, used this fear and envy as a tool of oppression for thousands of years. This explains much of the history of "mankind" over the last several millennia.

Taoists venerate the yin, the valley spirit, the primordial woman, as opposed to modern religions which were founded by and are presided over by men who maintain that the creator and sustainer of the universe is male. This has left little room for the female, other than as mother, virgin and bride.

The Tao of sex is a way of acknowledging the energetic superiority of the woman while training the man to be able to meet her on equal and solid ground, to their mutual benefit. As Jolan Chang says, "With the Tao, men and women can become true loving and equal partners, thus making the age-old conflict between the sexes a thing of the past."

This is accomplished primarily when a man understands the art of ejaculation control or *optional ejaculation*. We are all familiar with the post-lovemaking scenario in which the woman wants to sit up and talk and cuddle and perhaps continue with more lovemaking while the man, utterly exhausted and used up, rolls over and goes to sleep, leaving the woman frustrated, lonely and often angry. The man seems like an unfeeling, uncaring oaf, concerned only with his own pleasure and all too ready to drop out as soon as that pleasure is experienced. The seemingly oafish behavior is simply their bodies' reaction to what has just happened.

In order to understand what has happened, we need to know just what is involved in ejaculation and what it is that is ejaculated. Semen itself, according to Mantak Chia, contains "a treasure house of vitamins, minerals, trace elements, hormones, proteins, ions, enzymes, and other vital nutritional substances." This precious fluid is made up of nutrients taken from all parts of the body, being comprised of a large amount of cerebro-spinal fluid. "Every organ pays heavy tribute to the glands that produce the sexual seed," Chia says. "Because a single drop of semen houses such prodigious life energies, frequent loss of fluid depletes the body systems of their most precious nutrients and speeds the inevitable physical decline into old age." Not to mention sound sleep! Or, as Jolan Chang puts it, "He is not unlike a soldier in heavy fighting who suddenly realizes that he has used up all his ammunition."

Most men are all too familiar with a sudden empty feeling that happens immediately after ejaculation. But we have been taught that this feeling is normal. We become used to the idea that once we have attained orgasm we are no longer interested in sex. The woman who was so desirable and exciting minutes ago is suddenly almost too much to bear. We would like to just lie back and take it easy or perhaps take a short nap. But she, being a woman and slow to boil, is still bubbling away, ready to go on to new exciting heights, making us feel deficient and irritated.

This is not the way we would like to feel after a wonderful lovemaking session. A few short moments ago we felt juicy and electric and powerful. Now we feel like a deflated balloon. And what's just as bad, if not worse, is that that wonderful juicy, electric and powerful feeling only lasted a few minutes. It seems as though, just when we thought we were getting a handle on it, it slipped out from under us and left us washed up on the shore like a beached whale! Woman, being yin, or water, is slow to warm—in contrast to the male, who is yang, or fire, and who flares up immediately. The danger is that in his sudden flaring he will continue past the woman and leave her far behind, just as she is coming to a boil. We are left with the scenario of the lonely frustrated woman and the oafish sleeping man.

Taoist sex offers us a different scenario. The man goes slowly, matching his energy level to the woman's. They come to a slow or quick boil together. And instead of it being a rapid climb up the mountain with orgasm (especially the male's) as the peak goal, lovemaking becomes a goalless and joyful event, a marvelous dance between two people who are enjoying each other and themselves. It becomes more of a long, even sharing and less of a sudden peaking with an equally sudden drop.

Jolan Chang describes this type of lovemaking as "a pleasure of peace, not of violence, a sensual and lastingly satisfying melting into something larger and more transcendent than oneself. It is a feeling of wholeness, not of separation; a merging and a sharing, not an exclusive, private and lonely spasm."

Mantak Chia describes it even more poetically as follows:

When the exchange of *ching chi*(sexual energy) reaches a certain intensity and balance, the solid bodies of the two lovers begin pulsating as if charged with electricity. The feeling of having solid flesh disappears. You are suddenly a pillar of vibrating energy held in exquisite balance by your lover's field of energy. This is a total orgasm of body and soul. The battling ego shrinks to the true size, a tiny grain of sand, and reluctantly begins humming in chorus with the ocean of the subtle universe that rhythmically washes over it.

This type of lovemaking is not unique to Taoists, however. There is a long-standing tradition in Hindu tantric practices of saving the semen. And even in the West we have *coitus reservatus* or sex that is not interrupted by male climax. Louis W. Meldman, in an article on *Coitus Reservatus and Mystical Sex* writes:

> Because there is no accidental male sexual release in coitus reservatus, sex is not forced to end. Therefore this type of lovemaking provides the unhurried sexual *context* that allows lovers to become immersed in the endless immediate present moment, while their bodies spontaneously move together as one.

This technique was also used in Arabic, Gnostic and other European cultures. Many men, in all ages and cultures, have stumbled upon this technique by themselves and have found that it works for them.

Many of the ancient Taoists equated losing semen or *jing* with losing the essence of life itself. Sun S'su-Mo, the great Chinese physician who lived during the Tang dynasty, said, "When a man squanders his semen, he will be sick and if he carelessly exhausts his semen he will die. And for a man this is the most important point to remember." Mantak Chia writes:

> The ejaculatory orgasm to which most men are so deeply attached restricts their life force to the genitals. . . .Frequent ejaculation is an infantile attempt to solve our lonely separation from bliss.

To Come or Not to Come

> *One who retains his seed increasingly respects every form of life.*
> Mantak Chia

> *Effective conservation of the life force energy and its gradual transformation into a kind of spiritual/material substance is both the birthright and responsibility of mankind.*
> Mantak Chia

> *The term orgasm does not appear in the Tao. Its terms are enjoyment and satisfaction.*
> Jolan Chang

At first, the idea of giving up the orgasm is very difficult for most men, if not downright impossible. After all, isn't that what sex is all about? Not to mention that while it is considered harmful for the man to ejaculate, it is not harmful for the woman! This is because when men have orgasms or ejaculate they do just that—ejaculate their semen outside their body. And while there are many nutritious and magical properties to this substance for the woman, he loses it all. When a woman has an orgasm she injaculates, and all her secretions, or most of them, stay within her body, to be reabsorbed into her own system.

"Not fair!" cries the man. Not only is the woman the repository of inexhaustible yin and because of it, energetically superior to the man, but she gets to come and he doesn't! But some Taoist teachers say women should also control their need to have orgasms. After all, if we are trying to get the man to let go of his goal orientation toward lovemaking, it's only right that the woman, too, works on the same thing. While it is not actually as physiologically harmful for the woman to come as the man, if they want to truly meet on the same level, she also needs to give a little in this department. This will, of course, be entirely up to the individual woman and her partner.

So the main emphasis here, as it is in most Taoist writings, will be on the man's role. Mantak Chia and his wife Maneewan have written an excellent book about the woman's side of all this, called *Healing Love Through the Tao: Cultivating Female Sexual Energy*, which is full of exercises and techniques for women.

For men, sex without the release of orgasm seems like a joyless and uninteresting affair at first. But don't knock it till you've tried it! It takes a little practice and a lot of trusting and surrendering, but it's well worth it. And the new levels of experience it opens up are just as exciting, if not more so, than the old way of lovemaking. But the key word here is "surrender."

As Daniel P. Reid says:

Taoists advocate living in complete harmony with the great patterns of nature, and they venerate womanhood precisely because women are by nature far closer to the primordial powers of the cosmos than men. There is no place for male chauvinism, practical or philosophical, in Taoist tradition. A man who clearly understands the nature of a woman's sexual superiority has already taken the first step towards utilizing that superior power. All he needs to do is to practice the proper skills. But a man who denies nature and defies Tao will wilt and perish before his time, no matter how chauvinistically he preens and prances.

It is in the act of surrendering to his partner and to the discipline of lovemaking without ejaculation that the man has the chance to surrender to the Tao itself. Remember, Taoists are eminently practical. They developed a way to use sex as a tool and a practice for communication, communion, self-awareness, energy exchange and personal health. All for the same price!

For a man to surrender, both to his partner and to the moment they are sharing, may be a challenge, but in doing so, that precious moment is expanded and carried over into the rest of his, and his partner's, lives. As Jolan Chang says, "A couple who can make love ecstatically together are likely to have provided each other with peace and harmony in every way and hence their loving and attraction for each other may increase and become a more permanent one." When he surrenders—to the moment of sharing, the moment of yielding, the moment of physical and psychic attunement, with his partner as well as within himself—the man has the opportunity to expand both within and without to the greater moment, the greater union, the greater attunement—to what we call Tao.

This of course applies to the woman as well, though perhaps without as much struggle. She too is able to relax, to forget about performing, about pleasing her partner at a cost to herself. She too is able to let go and feel her own energy move within her body and then out and into her partner's. Together they form a double helix as their combined energies spiral into and out of each other. As such, the couple experience the Taoist notion that the universe itself is "the intercourse of the yin and yang energy of nature which brings about human life."

Earlier I mentioned *optional ejaculation*. Just how is this accomplished? As with all Taoist practices, it is really quite simple, but needs a little practice. To begin with, the man pays close attention to when he is reaching "the point of no return" or when he is close to ejaculation. Then, he simply stops thrusting and, keeping himself still within his partner, breathes deeply and slowly until he feels ready to resume thrusting again. The key is to be able to be sensitive enough to his body to be able to tell when he is reaching the "point of no return" without going past it.

Taoist sexual practices require a high level of sensitivity on both sides. Cultivating one's sensitivity not only heightens the levels of pleasure and response in each partner, but also sensitizes each partner to the other. It is not possible to learn Taoist sexual practices without first cultivating this level of sensitivity in both partners.

As in all energy practices, the idea is to go slowly, especially in the beginning. It's difficult to be sensitive to what's really happening in your body when you're going eighty miles an hour. This slower pace, besides allowing you the space to feel what is going on in your body, also slows down the whole lovemaking session, allowing it to go on much longer. According to the Kinsey Report, three quarters of all men in the United States ejaculate within two minutes or less! Then we're back to the scenereo of the slow to boil woman being left behind by the quick to flame out man.

In Taoist lovemaking, the man matches his energy with the woman's, slowly and steadily, so that they may be able to arrive at a mutual level of satisfaction together. Sometimes that may consist of or include orgasm in one or both partners, sometimes not. What people find in this style of lovemaking is that the need for the physical release of orgasm becomes less of a pressure and more of an option.

By going slowly and being sensitive to just what is going on in his body, the man is usually able to postpone his ejaculation. It is often helpful to constrict the anus and pull up on the testicles, thereby sealing off that area from leakage. Holding the breath for a moment or so, until the urge to ejaculate is over, is also helpful. Another option is to put pressure on the urethra (the tube through which the semen travels) itself by pressing the point halfway between the anus and the scrotum, what Steven T. Chang calls "The Million Dollar Point." By pressing with two or three fingers directly on this point, (known in Chinese medicine as Conception Vessel 1), just prior to ejaculation, the man can cause the semen to remain within the body instead of losing it outside of himself. At the very least, this practice will cut down measurably on the amount of semen ejaculated and the commensurate energy loss.

Eventually, after much practice in sensitivity and mind and breath control, the adept is able to stop ejaculation without physical intervention. At this point he is able to begin transforming sexual energy into spiritual energy.

To Taoists, sex is merely energy, and, as such, it can be used or abused. As energy, it can be used for pleasure, for communion, for communication, and for health benefits. Because it is an extremely potent form of energy, it can also be used for spiritual cultivation. The notion that one has to be celibate in order to lead a spiritual life was never given any credence by Taoists, until the later Buddhist influence crept into religious Taoism. But the true natural philosophy of Tao has never felt a need to cut itself off from such a primal source of energy and delight. "Sexual energy," says Mantak Chia, "offers a link between our biological and metaphysical indentities, between the animal and the divine."

Another problem with enforced celibacy is that disregarding a particular function of the body creates problems for the system as a whole. Medical autopsies on over a thousand Catholic priests have shown that one third of them died of prostate complications or prostate cancer. Also, the practice of celibacy in women brings on eventual deterioration of the sexual organs caused by long term congestion in the ovaries and breasts, in turn affecting the internal organs.

Mantak Chia advises us:

> Cultivating sex energy is important in nourishing your spirit, but without proper diet, exercise, meditation, virtuous moral behavior and love, true cultivation is impossible. Likewise, don't ignore sex and focus excessively on the higher spiritual centers; the roof will easily fall without a strong foundation.

How often a man may safely ejaculate depends on a variety of factors such as age, level of general health and even the time of year. For instance, in the summer, when the air is warm or hot, a man may ejaculate much more often than in the winter when he needs more vital energy to keep his body warm. Also, if his health is good he will not suffer the loss of energy so much as if he is in poor health or a weak state due to injury or medical intervention.

The old Taoists came up with all sorts of other formulas such as the following from Sun S'su Mo, a very famous physician who was born in 581 CE and lived to be 101 years old:

> A man of twenty can have one emission every four days. A man of thirty can have one emission in every eight days. A man of forty can have one emission in every ten days. A man of fifty can have one emission every twenty days. A man of sixty should no longer emit. If he is exceptionally strong and healthy he can still have one emission monthly.

There were however, several admonitions about when not to engage in sex. It was taught that in times of great seismic or meteorological disturbance the qi or electromagnetic energy in the air can be very disturbing to our own personal qi or energy system, so making love during these times is not conducive to good energetic control and sharing. There was also an injunction against making love while intoxicated or under extreme emotional conditions. It would be very difficult to remain sufficiently sensitive, both to one's self and to one's partner at such a time.

There is leeway for each individual to find his own rate of emission, without necessarily using a lot of complicated formulas. Experiment and find out for yourself what works for you. Taoists should never submit to rigid, dogmatic codes of any sort, but explore within reasonable boundaries in order to find out just what is right for their personal cultivation.

Above all, don't be daunted by the seeming difficulty of this method of lovemaking. It will take a little while to master, so don't worry or get too frustrated with yourself for "blowing it," especially at the beginning. It may even feel a little awkward and unnatural at first but once you get the hang of it, it will seem extremely natural and simple. The willingness to try something new, and the cooperation of your partner (extremely important) will help you on your way to becoming a "seminal kung fu" master.

Daniel P. Reid says, "Despite its novelty in light of conventional sensuality, ejaculation control is really as natural as breathing and flexing the muscles." But let's not forget that sex involves at least two people. Which takes us to our next section.

The Clouds and the Rain

Of all things that make man prosper none can be compared to sexual intercourse. It is modeled after Heaven and takes its pattern by earth, it regulates Yin and rules Yang. Those who understand its significance can nurture their nature and prolong their years; those who miss its true meaning will harm themselves and die before their time.
Master Tung Hsuan

When two people love each other consciously their energies are intentionally consecrated to the good of humanity. This kind of love offering develops a special egolessness in the lovers and will inspire others whom they meet.
Mantak Chia

Sex is probably the most loaded word in our language. For many people it is such an overwhelming and difficult subject that they don't even know where to begin with it. Sex, or what passes for sex, permeates Western society and is used to sell everything from cars to politics. Sex is talked about and written about and even sung about more than any other subject, yet most people still know appallingly little about it. Mostly what people are talking about, writing about and singing about is the *idea* of sex. And this *idea* has become so complicated and convoluted that hardly anyone has a clue as to what sex is really about.

Some may view sex as a great mysterious and tangled area, full of pitfalls and danger. Others think of sex as something exciting, titillating, powerful, or frightening. Sometimes it's regarded as all of these things simultaneously. An unreal image of what is sexy and provocative is fed to us by the media, causing most people to feel they don't measure up. They know deep down inside that they will never achieve the level of perfection and glamour pictured for them by the media, and they feel cheated, angry, depressed, frightened, and powerless.

This *idea* of sex steals people's sense of personal power, self respect and self love. In their anger and despondency over what they perceive to be their own and their partner's sexuality, many people act out in violent or unhealthy ways. The rise of sexual abuse, especially of children, is indicative of that anger. Many people can only feel sexually powerful with someone much smaller or less powerful. In the past it is has been brought to bear on women, who were seen as "the weaker sex." Not all women are content to be the weaker sex these days, and so the children suffer.

The *idea* of sex and sexuality can be overwhelming, mysterious and terrifying. So many layers of morality and control and misunderstood emotional garbage are built into it that it is no wonder many people have such a hard time with it. And our society's emphasis on the rush, the high, the peak experience hasn't helped any. Sex has become a commodity, bought and sold just like any other commodity, and is one of the biggest industries in the world, built on greed, abuse and control.

Taoist sexual practices offer an alternative to this scenario, one that is healthy and positive. The man serves the woman, giving her primacy over him. There is a continued sharing of energy, trust, intimacy and pleasure between both partners, and emphasis is placed on safe and healthy sexual practices that can build energy rather than tear it down. In today's world of deadly sexually transmitted diseases it is even more important to practice "safe" sex than ever before. That is, sex that does not spread diseases, does not drain the body of needed energy and vitality, and that is based, mutually, on love and respect.

In ancient China, human love, expressed through sexuality, was seen as the most potent medicine you could take. It was a kind of 'human herb' that could cure most ailments as it restored the flow of qi which governs our organ vitality and general immunological system. During the Tang dynasty (618–906 CE), the Art of the Bedroom was even classified as a branch of Chinese medicine.

This is accomplished in part when the male partner practices optional ejaculation and aligns himself energetically with the woman. In addition, when we make love, there is an important and dynamic exchange of fluids as well as energy. The old phrase *clouds and rain*, which was used in ancient times to describe the sexual act, refers to the clouds as the ova of the earth and rain as the sperm of heaven. Thus the sexual act was seen as a sort of grand dance wherein two people not only shared their own love and vitality but enacted the cosmic dance which enables all life to grow.

The terms used for sexuality and sexual organs testify to the playful and poetic attitude of the ancient Taoists. Terms such as Jade Gate and Cinnabar Cleft for the vagina, Jade Terrace and Precious Pearl for the clitoris, Inner gate for the cervix, and Golden Valley for the vulva are all indicative of this attitude. Jolan Chang lists eight names for the eight depths or "valleys" of the vagina alone, including Lute-String for the depth of one inch, Water-Chestnut Teeth for the level of two inches, Inner Door for the level of seven inches, and North Pole for the level of eight inches!

While there are numberless names for a woman's sexual anatomy there are only a few, such as Jade Stem and Turtle Head, for the man's special parts. This is in keeping with the deep veneration for women which plays such a large part in Taoist thought and attitude.

Taoists say that it takes seven years to know the rhythms of woman's body, seven years to learn her mind, and seven years to understand her spirit. How many men are willing or able to put in this kind of time to truly and deeply understand his partner?

The women's movement of the last twenty-five years or so has made it very clear just what it is women want from men and also what it is they do not want. Women do want self empowerment, a feeling of co-responsibility with their partner along with accountability, a sense of self worth that is not based on glamour or how much value they possess in the sexual marketplace, a feeling of mutual trust and intimacy, and the knowledge that they are accepted for whom and what they really are.

This is just what the Tao of sex is all about! Taoist sexual practices are really not possible without a deep sense of trust and in turn, the intimacy which that trust generates. Mantak Chia says, "For many American men, sexuality actually remains on an infantile level. It is often no more than an extension of feeding." When a man practices the Tao of sex he is acknowledging that what he and his partner are doing is worth a little work, a little effort, a small amount of self control, in order for them both to reach even higher levels of ecstasy, communion and communication. And the woman is acknowledging that she is willing to support and help him with this achievement, for both their sakes.

The Poetry of Passion

The Taoists, being practical, propose that a man can begin with the most accessible energy at hand, namely the sexual attraction between men and women, and use that as a springboard to more subtle realms.
Mantak Chia

The man sacrifices a small measure of short-term pleasure in return for the long-term benefits of health and longevity, while the woman enjoys complete unrestricted sexual pleasure in exchange for a measure of her abundant

supplies of life-prolonging essence and energy.
Daniel P. Reid

The poetry of passion begins with the premise that sexuality is as much a part of spirituality as meditation. As we have seen, Taoists view sexuality as both sacred and healthy, if expressed in a sacred and healthy manner. Central to this is the concept of the feminine as stronger than the masculine. The ancient Taoist ideal of the feminine nature of the earth was of paramount importance in the development of Taoist thought.

To the ancient Chinese, sex was an art form, as subtle and illuminating as a fine painting. As Daniel Reid says: "The Chinese view sex as a basic human function similar to eating, sleeping, and so forth, and they cultivate it as an art and a pleasure, as well as an adjunct to health and longevity."

As mentioned earlier, the very terms used for sexual intercourse and sexual organs are different than the ones we are used to. They are poetic and descriptive, even playful. The idea that sex was something shameful or immoral was unheard of to the Taoists. It is interesting that among the extremely widespread erotic literature of ancient China (much of which was suppressed in later times by Buddhists and Confucians) we find almost no mention of sadism or masochism. Instead, much of it is spent on elaborate descriptions of varied and often highly intricate and imaginative lovers' trysts.

As for masturbation, Taoist thought is a little different than many current ideas. While Taoists would never judge masturbation from a *moral* standpoint, *energetically* it is regarded as a waste. Once again, it is a bit different for the man than for the woman. Since the man ejaculates his essence outside his body, the idea of expelling his seed into an empty void is a waste of valuable energy. But since the woman injaculates, she doesn't lose her precious energy. Hence it is not seen as a problem for the woman.

Oddly enough, a lot of the old wives' tales of excessive masturbation leading to blindness, memory loss and other mental problems are upheld in Taoist medicine. The same rules apply here as in a man ejaculating too often during sex.

Another problem Taoists have with masturbation is that no exchange occurs—there is no sharing, no communion with another. As Jolan Chang says: "Masturbation is a poor substitute, and we should treat it as a last resort when no love partner is available. To masturbate is a lonely endeavor, devoid of human warmth, contact, and communication. In the language of the Tao, it lacks the harmony of Yin and Yang."

On the subject of same-gender sex, Taoists would never judge homosexual practices from a moral standpoint, but are more concerned about an imbalance of energy. Two yins or two yangs together make it harder to attain a proper yin/yang balance. Fortunately, there are practices that one can do to remedy the situation. A partner in a male same-sex couple needs to make sure he is getting yin energy from somewhere else in his life, either from contact with women friends, practices that evoke the earth or yin nature in himself, and certain yin-building herbs. Likewise, a partner in a female same-sex couple needs to make sure she is receiving enough yang essence in the same way. This subject is beyond the scope of this work but suffice it to say there are ways of achieving balance, though it does take a little extra effort.

Ancient China had a much different social structure than we do now. It was a polygamous culture in which men (who could afford it) had multiple wives and concubines. The sexual act itself often consisted of several partners. Indeed, some postures even require three or more participants just to perform them!

But in today's culture the idea of multiple partners not only complicates things emotionally but energetically as well. Mantak Chia says: "If you think you can love two women at once, be ready to spend double the chi to transform and balance their energy. I doubt if many men can really do that and feel deep security." I'm sure the same goes for women and two or more men. Later on he says, "For your own sake do not abandon your integrity for the sake of physical pleasure or the pretense that you are doing deep spiritual exercises. If you sleep with one woman you don't love, your subtle energies will not be in balance and psychic warfare can begin."

Although there are currently many books and workshops available on tantra, some don't stress enough the responsibility that this path requires. Mantak Chia warns, "If you feel unable to use your sexual power lovingly, then do not use it at all! Sex is a gleaming, sharp, two-edged sword, a healing tool that can quickly become a weapon."

Too often sexuality is used as power, usually over someone else. But this two-edged sword can easily be turned on one's self. This is not the way of Tao. It is not the way of eternal integrity and unity. It only leads to disaster. The energies and powers accrued through any spiritual practice, especially sexual ones, are never to be used to dominate another or simply to benefit one's self at the expense of someone else. As Van Gulik writes:

> The Taoist speculations on the magical power of the sexual union applied to both man and woman. Although there were some Taoist adepts who selfishly concentrated on strengthening their own vital force by tapping that of

their woman-partners, disregarding their health and sometimes even harming it, the general principle was that both partners should share in the benefits accruing from the sexual discipline. Indeed Taoism has been on the whole much more considerate to woman, and has given much more thought to her physical and emotional needs than Confucianism ever did.

In the Tao of sex there is not only an emotional and physical exchange but an equally important and vital exchange of energy through the exchange of bodily fluids. We have already talked about the need for the man to control his ejaculation. One of the reasons for him to not conserve himself totally is that when he does ejaculate into his woman partner she can absorb his precious fluid through the extremely porous membranes of her vagina. Thus he gives her an infusion of nourishing yang essence which she then combines with her own innate yin to bring herself into a more harmonious balance.

Not only that, but when a woman has an orgasm she too "ejaculates" her own precious substance which the man can absorb through his own organ, also very porous, especially at the head. In this way he receives an infusion of her precious yin essence, which he then combines with his own innate yang in order to bring himself into an equally harmonious balance.

While it depletes a man each time he gives up his precious substance, it does not deplete the woman to give up hers. Instead she is able to give her essence generously without loss to herself. This is another reason that the man is encouraged to bring the woman to complete fulfillment as often as he can, while controlling himself in the process. In this way he will conserve his own precious essence while absorbing hers.

If this doesn't seem quite fair to the woman, who is giving up her essence without receiving his, remember that energetically the woman is far stronger than the man, and an occasional infusion of yang is usually sufficient to keep her happy and healthy. In the meantime she has her man working most diligently to make sure she reaches fulfillment as often as possible!

It is only through a prolonged and emotionally bonded relationship that this kind of practice can succeed. It is crucial for the man to work with a partner who supports him in this practice. Otherwise it will be too easy for the woman to "push him over the edge." She too must be willing to open to this practice herself if her partner is ever going to succeed. With occasional exceptions, she may decide at some point to "give up" her own orgasm so that for her too lovemaking is a goalless act.

After a man and woman are able to gain some measure of control over their energy and in turn enter into a heightened state of awareness and experience with one another, what to do with all this great juicy sexual energy? Fortunately, the Taoists have an answer. Remember, sexual energy is just that, energy. It is part of the kidney system, where jing is stored and reproductive energy is produced. When we have built up lots of sexual energy without dissipating it we are healthy, juicier, and more dynamic human beings. People around us notice this. We are more magnetic and desirable, sexually, but also personally and even professionally. This great energy we have built up can be used for many things besides the sexual act itself. It can be channeled into all sorts of creative and business endeavors. It is up to us to use this energy in whatever way we wish.

Another way we can use it is in self cultivation. We can circulate this energy throughout our bodies, using it to heal and strengthen organs, tissue and blood, and qi pathways. We can use it to open up spiritual and psychic centers. The energy or qi in our body travels in very specific pathways, the two largest being up the spine and down the front of the body. This sexual energy cannot only be circulated within your own body but also between your partner and you. In this way both become a living tai chi symbol, embodying the eternal dance of yin and yang in all its beauty and glory. This practice, called the microcosmic orbit, is best learned by working with a teacher. It is very old and unique to Taoism; it is simple yet powerful.

This kind of energy circulation, besides having both health and spiritual benefits, can also affect the aging process itself. Mantak Chia says:

> Much evidence points to the link between harmonious sexual activity and the retardation of aging. Loving sex stimulates high-quality hormonal secretion. The presence of these hormones in the blood appears to slow the aging process. With Taoist cultivation one produces unusually potent hormones because one focuses energy effectively on the endocrine glands, stimulating them to much greater levels of activity. Because the hormone energy is constantly circulated within the body instead of being ejaculated, a successful student of Taoist loving finds himself with ever-increasing amounts of energy as he grows older.

The main thing to remember is that Taoist sexual practices can be powerful tools for a greater sense of well being, physical and emotional as well as spiritual. They also engender a high level of commitment and self responsibility. The idea is not merely to become a great sexual athlete, or to use other people to enhance your own vitality. These practices instead make possible much deeper levels of trust, communion and communication than you ever thought possible. Use them well and you will be rewarded amply.

Chapter Sources

Daniel P. Reid, *The Tao of Health, Sex and Longevity*
Stephen T. Chang, *The Tao of Sexology*
R.H. Van Gulik, *Sexual Life in Ancient China*
Jolan Chang, *The Tao of Love and Sex*
Jolan Chang, *The Tao of the Loving Couple*
Mantak Chia, *Male Sexual Energy*
Louis W. Meldman, *Coitus Reservatus and Mystical Sex*
    (Gnosis Magazine, Fall 1990)
Hua Ching Ni, *Essence of Universal Spirituality*
Mantak and Maneewan Chia, *Healing Love Through the Tao:
    Cultivating Female Sexual Energy*

13

Tao and the Great Mother

The universal Mother is the origin of the untraceable formless energy, it is called Tao.
Hua-Ching Ni

The women's wisdom is that if you go deep into the earth, your body, it will lift you into heaven.
Mantak Chia

While other religions exhort their believers to war against and transcend the earthly conditions, the Tao Te Ching regards the earth as the abode of Tao.
Ellen M. Chen

The Taoist emphasis on the Great Mother is rooted in antiquity. In its exaltation of the Tao as the primordial womb, we see how different this path is from the male focused and dominated religions of the world.

The Valley Spirit or the Mysterious Female symbolizes the richness and fecundity of the Tao, ever rebirthing in an endless manifestation of creativity. The Primal Valley symbolizes the image of the Tao as the empty vessel, used but never exhausted. To rephrase an old saying, primal qi can never be destroyed, only changed, redirected. As Hua-Ching Ni says:

The Universal Mother comes from the interplay of formless and form, nothingness or something, non-being and being. The Universal Mother is the origin of the formless and formed. She is nothingness or non-being. Thus she is the source of all things and all being. Thus, the entirety of the universe is the Universal Mother.

Ancient Taoists believed that humans were born of a combination of star dust and earth elements. In other words, we are literally children of the earth, aligned internally and eternally with her elemental energies and forms. It is in the conscious relationship with the Great Mother within us as well as our ongoing and sacred relationship with the earth itself that we, as Taoists, can best hold true to that sacred trust.

Know the yang but hold to the yin, says Lao Tzu. Know the important creative power of the yang but do not let go of the enormously creative power of the yin, the dark, mysterious, watery womb of our origin.

Carl Jung, that natural Taoist, wrote:

I would not speak ill of our relation to good Mother earth...he who is rooted in the soil endures. Alienation from the unconscious and from its historical conditions spells rootlessness. That is the danger that lies in wait for the conqueror of foreign lands, and for every individual who, through one-sided allegiance to any kind of -ism, loses touch with the dark, maternal, earthy ground of his being.

With their emphasis on the yin, the essential maternal, feminine energy of the universe, Taoists have always supported women's rights and privileges, even as Chinese culture became dominated by Confucianism, a system that is inherently anti-feminine. Under Confucianism, women, with their mutilated feet, were house-bound, uneducated, and had no voice in politics, society or even life outside their tightly bound world.

According to Charles Humana and Wang Wu:

The Nu-chieh (The Ideal Woman), an early Confucian work, began by asserting that woman's subservience should be established at birth and that the female child, as a mark of the parents' contrition, should immediately be hidden under the bed. They should then fast for three days and offer prayers to the ancestral gods. The female child's early education and training should be devoted to fitting her to serve her menfolk, and for this modesty and obedience were the highest virtues. She should walk backward from any room in which men were present, and the thought of comparing should never be allowed to pass through her head. The secret of acquiring such humility was to regard herself as always being wrong in any dispute, and to feel herself lucky if she avoided severe punishment.

How far they strayed from the teachings of Lao Tzu and Chuang Tzu, who respected and even venerated the superiority of the yin over the yang! Thomas Cleary, in an excellent book on the secret teachings of Taoist women, *Immortal Sisters*, tells us:

Among religious traditions that surveyed, or followed, the widespread transitions from matriarchal to patriarchal society in ancient times, Taoism is probably unique in having a feminine element that is intrinsic to the religion and whose traces are not only clearly identifiable but indeed indelible, in both esoteric and exoteric teachings, reflected in both myth and history, manifest in both theory and practice.

He goes on to say:

...it was considered especially easy for women to attain the essence of Taoism even under the rigorous conditions of patriarchal society.

And that:

Politically and socially, Taoism never definitively overcame the repressive use of orthodoxy on more than local scales, but it did always provide women and other oppressed groups with opportunities for education and psychical growth traditionally denied them by Confucian establishment.

There were, and continue to be great female masters of qigong, tai ji and Taoist internal alchemy. While it takes a combination of yin and yang to complete the circle, women, because of their intrinsic yin nature, were always looked upon as naturally close to Tao and better able to fuse the inner yin and yang to produce the Golden Embryo of spiritual immortality.

Perhaps the unique teachings of Tao as regards to women and the Great Mother image can best be explained in the following story.

Like A Flower Unfolding

The woman, sitting still and quiet in her little hut at the foot of the mountain, was old, even ancient. She had lived alone in her small home for more years than she could remember. She had come when she was a young woman, barely out of childhood, to escape an unwanted marriage, something quite unheard of in her time. But she had always been a stubborn and willful child, full of questions about everything under heaven.

"Where do dead people go when they die?" she had asked her father when her beloved grandmother died. The air had been thick with incense and the chanting of the Buddhist monks. Her father had sat upright and stiff at the edge of the room while his mother was chanted into the next world. His daughter sat next to him, fidgeting constantly, trying to see through the haze of incense to where her grandmother lay, stiff and so quiet. "Will I see her again, baba?" she had asked.

Her father had turned to her and hissed, "Be quiet. Do not ask so many questions; it is unseemly." Her father had been a strict Confucianist and did not like to talk about the dead. Confucius had taught that it was bad for men to talk of ghosts and spirits. Better to keep one's attention to the world of solid reality and all the myriad rules of relationship and composure.

She had insisted and was finally sent from the room. But that had not stopped her questions. "Why is the sky so blue and the earth so brown?" she asked her mother. Her mother, who worked all the time it seemed, had no time for useless questions from a silly girl and always found chores for her to do when she asked such questions. But even that had not stopped her.

"Why can my brothers study and learn to read and write but girls cannot?" she had asked. "Why must mama work all the time, day and night, while baba sits in the courtyard drinking tea and spitting watermelon seeds with his friends? How is it that big brother can learn to fight with the sword and spear and I cannot? Why, when we go to the temple to burn incense and kowtow to the gods, can we not hear their answer? Why do they say that Lady Kuan Yin hears all prayers yet she allowed nainai to die? Why do the gods allow the rain to stop and the fields dry up and blow away? Why will no one listen to me?" she cried loud and often.

The young girl was often punished for her incessant questions. "Do not question the natural order of things," she was told. "It has been this way for all of time and will be this way for all of time to come. You are a girl and so have already been shown disfavor by heaven," her mother explained. "You must not question, you must learn how to behave yourself like a proper lady."

Beginning on her thirteenth birthday she was given lessons from a book called the *Nu-chieh*. She learned that she should always submit to the males in the family and never allow any male outside of the household to behold her face. She was never to question the authority of the males in her family—first her father, her brothers and, ultimately, her husband and even her sons. She was to keep her head lowered in a room of males and to exit the room backward, with a meek and shuffling step.

This infuriated her. She didn't really know why. All the women of her family accepted this guidance without question. It was their lot in life, they understood. It was heaven's will that men should rule over women. It was nature's and heaven's law.

Her name was Chen Hua. Chen was her family name and Hua, or Flower, was her personal name. When her parents had named her, they had expected her to be a delicate and submissive flower but they had ended up with a thorny, prickly one. No amount of punishment or lecturing seemed to make any difference.

Finally, in exasperation, they decided to marry her off as soon as possible. Perhaps the strong and stern influence of a husband was what she needed. She would, of course, move into his home and be under the power of his mother, her mother-in-law. Perhaps *she* could force some sense into this stubborn and willful girl.

It was not that her parents did not love her, but they worried that her stubborn attitude would only cause her misery in life and so wanted to spare her further suffering. They truly felt that if she would only learn to let go of her own ideas and submit to the will of heaven and become a good submissive wife, she would be more likely to have a happy life.

When Chen Hua heard them planning her marriage to a neighboring farmer, a man twice her age and ugly to boot, she was furious. She would not submit to this, she vowed. But what could she do? Her parents had complete authority over her life. She couldn't just march in and defy them. It was unheard of. They could lock her in her room without food for as long as it took for her to yield. They could beat her or even kill her if they wanted without being punished by the authorities. After all, she was only a girl, and a disobedient one at that.

So she decided to run away. In those days she was fearless, and with the ignorance of youth she didn't think about the dangers in the wide and unknown world. She wrapped a few clothes and a ball of cold rice in a head scarf and stole out of her family's compound in the dead of night. No one would ever have imagined her doing such a thing and it was late morning before anyone would even notice she was gone. She intended to be far away by then.

Her destination was a distant mountain, a Taoist mountain. She knew that if she could manage to get that far the Taoists would take her in. She had met one once when her mother had taken her to the temple to offer prayers for a good harvest. Chen Hua has always loved the statue of the Lady Kuan Yin, even if she did let her nainai die. Kuan Yin herself had been a headstrong young girl once and had been deified to become a goddess, "She Who Hears The Cries Of The World." Chen Hua loved to light incense in front of the goddess and look up into the beautiful face with its slight smile, the smile of love and compassion for the whole world. The goddess held a small flask of heavenly nectar in one hand—one drop of which was said to cure anyone of any disease or pain—and her other hand was folded in a gesture of benediction and blessing.

While mother was speaking with the head priest and Chen Hua was happily gazing up at the calm, beautiful face of the goddess, a Taoist monk plunked himself down beside her. Unlike the Buddhist monks she was used to, his head was not shaved. His hair was long and a bit matted, coiled up in a loose knot on the top of his head and held with an ancient jade pin. His robe was very dusty and a bit ragged and he gave off the pleasant smell of pine trees and earth.

She, of course, did not speak to him or even look at him except out of the corner of her eye. Presently the Taoist looked over at her and, gesturing with his chin to the goddess, said "What do you think, is she pleased with all the incense and kowtowing everyone does to her?"

Chen Hua was confused. What had he meant by that? Of course the goddess would be pleased. That is what goddesses wanted, wasn't it? To be worshipped and sacrificed to. She decided to ignore this dirty, dusty Taoist and didn't bother to answer.

The Taoist turned away from the goddess then and, crossing his legs, appeared to go into a deep meditative trance. His breathing became very deep and slow; his abdomen enlarged to an alarming size when he breathed in and then shrank back in so far on his exhale that Chen Hua, out of the corner of her eye, could imagine his ribs sticking out.

Presently he opened his eyes and said, without looking around at her, "You know, all your questions do have answers. It's just that no one around here knows them."

Chen Hua jumped. How did he know about all her questions? She couldn't help but turn around and look at him. He still sat with his back to her, breathing in that deep yet forceful way. She regarded him a moment, a little afraid yet very curious.

He spoke up again. "There is a place where all your questions can be answered. Of course it is a bit far and for a girl, quite impossible to reach."

"What do you mean?" asked Chen Hua, her innate stubbornness asserting itself. "Just because I'm a girl doesn't mean that I can't do whatever I want to do!"

The Taoist chuckled to himself. "Of course, of course," he said. "I only meant that for *most* girls it is impossible. For some it is not only possible but of vital importance. Otherwise how can they ever hope to attain Tao?"

What did this strange monk mean by "attain Tao"? thought Chen Hua. She had never heard of such a thing. When her father spoke of Tao he meant the natural order of filial relationship, which usually ended up meaning the submissivness of women to men. She was not interested in that Tao. She had never heard her father mention anything about attaining Tao, he usually talked more about submitting to Tao. But perhaps this ragged monk meant something different.

She decided to admit to her ignorance, something she always found difficult to do. "What do you mean by this Tao that you speak of attaining?" she asked. When the Taoist turned around and smiled at her she felt relieved. He was not making fun of her, she decided.

"I'm afraid that to try to put the Tao into words is like trying to catch the wind in a jar. You may hold up the jar and try to catch some of the wind in it, but when you open it later you will find that it is empty. Anyone who tries to explain Tao in words will end up with an empty jar in the end. Tao is something that must be experienced, not explained."

They sat and talked for a long time. The Taoist, who appeared to be very young but spoke as someone with much life experience, explained to the young girl that asking questions was fine as long as one was prepared to accept the answers when they came. The best answers came from Nature, or better yet, from within one's own self, deep within where the true Self Nature dwelt.

He told her a little more about the Taoist community in the mountains where anyone was accepted as a student, male or female. It was difficult to reach, he said, and only someone of strong heart and spirit could get there. But if they succeeded, there was no end to the answers that could be found there.

She had been able to get only vague directions before her mother arrived to whisk her away from this strange, hairy man. That night Chen Hua lay awake for a long time, wondering what it would be like to live in a place where she could ask any questions she wanted and where she would be treated equally as a boy.

She was determined to find out, because that is exactly where she was going. She was not going to spend the rest of *her* life waiting on her husband and her sons, never allowed to have a thought of her own. She wouldn't let herself be sold into marriage to an old man who would do heaven knows what to her young body to satisfy his own male lust. She was going to reach this mountain and find these Taoists if she died trying.

She almost did die trying, too. It was a long journey for one so young. Countless times she yearned to give up, to just let go and die and be done with the endless torture of exhaustion and fear and hunger that followed her on the days of her journey. She begged and argued and even stole a few times to survive but she finally arrived with her virtue intact. She was so near death from exhaustion and starvation that the Taoists who discovered her outside the temple gate early one morning were roused to pity one who had obviously given so much of herself to find them.

Chen Hua spent the following days resting and eating the strong herbal broths the Taoists prepared for her. One, a young woman who was called Willow, spent much time with her, explaining the ways of the Taoist community. She listened to Chen Hua's many questions about what it was they did there, how they did it and why they did it and had tried to answer as many of them as she could. But most, she explained, would have to be answered by Chen Hua herself and that would take time and effort and much, much patience.

Oddly, this made sense to Chen Hua, so she stopped her ceaseless questioning and decided to watch and listen, seeing how much she could understand for herself.

After she felt strong again she was introduced to the rest of the community and formally welcomed. The abbess was an old woman with a still-thick bun of white hair pinned to the top of her head. Willow told her that the abbess was over ninety years old although she looked scarcely older than Chen Hua's own mother, who was in her early fifties. Abbess White Pine welcomed Chen Hua to their community high above the world and told her she could stay as long as she liked and would be taught anything she wanted to know.

This excited Chen Hua immensely. Before long she was sitting in classes with other young girls and boys, studying the words of Lao Tzu and Chuang Tzu and other ancient achieved ones. She began to learn the simple yet powerful movements, many based on animal movements, that the Taoists did to begin each day. She learned about qi, or primal energy, and how it moved through her body and how to produce a stronger and more vital current with the use of specific herbs and movements.

She learned about the Immortal Sister Yu who taught herself Taoist breathing methods from an old book she had found. At the age of fourteen, she, like Chen Hua, ran away from an unwanted marriage and went into the mountains, to search for a legendary alchemical workshop. She was also told about Immortal Sister Zhang who healed people by projecting her own energy into them. There was also Wu Cailuan, the daughter of a Taoist adept—because of her great spiritual influence, her scholar husband retired from society himself and went off with her to pursue their spiritual cultivation. She studied the sacred writings of the great Taoist immortal Lu Dong-bin and his female disciple Ho Hsein-ku.

She was taught that, as serious students of the Way, men require nine years to attain immortality while women need only three. She learned that women were considered superior to men in the ways of the Tao, that their nature was water and their substance flowers. She was taught that women are represented by the hexagram in the ancient book of the I Ching (Yi Jing) as K'un, receptiveness, not, as she had been taught in her youth, submissiveness. K'un represents the virtues of the Earth. It is symbolized by the mare. It is primal yin energy and allows all things to become manifest.

She learned how to sit in meditation. Man's center is in the lower dan tien, in the lower abdomen, she was taught. Woman's center is between the breasts, the heart center. She was taught how to regulate her breath and calm her heart and concentrate on the *shan zhong* point, between the two breasts, just above the solar plexus. She was taught how to massage her breasts in various ways and for various numbers of circulation and then how to circulate the accumulated female energy through her waist and sexual organs and then throughout her body.

Later on she was taught more advanced practices such as "slaying the red dragon" in which she was able to stop her menses and circulate the energy that she had lost every month. Her complexion became soft and rosy and she remaining youthful for many years.

She learned how to go so far into herself that the border between what she thought of as her own personal self and that of the greater universal self was crossed and she felt herself expand into a feeling of spaciousness and grandness that she had never experienced before. She felt her own qi and that of the universal qi blend and become one in a way that allowed her to travel on the wings of light and receive answers to any question she cared to ask.

After a number of years passed she began to ask less and less and allow herself to receive more and more, naturally, effortlessly, and in that way she was able to relax into something close to Tao itself.

The Taoists were unique for their time because they received both men and women into their community, without discrimination. Indeed, they venerated the female, or yin aspect of life over the male, or yang aspect. Though they recognized that the universe consists of both, still they deferred to the female whenever they could. "Know the yang," they said, "but hold to the yin." They spoke often of the power of the soft to overcome the hard. They used water as an example, malleable to the extreme of taking whatever shape it was enclosed in, soft to the touch, yet capable of creating great canyons with its strength. They spoke of the power of patience, flexibility and surrender, surrender to the great and eternal Tao.

"Look to Nature," her teachers never tired of telling her. "Nature is the greatest teacher, greater than any book or any master. Observe the cycles of the seasons, watch how animals conduct themselves—how they move, how they rest, what they do when they are sick or injured."

"This planet we live on is alive," they told her. "She has intelligence and power. Send your roots down deep into her and draw up the pure yin qi. The stars are alive; they move amidst the spaces of the universe in great spiral dances. They are the source of yang qi. Each of us is a microcosm of the entire universe. Each of us is a planet, separate yet interrelated with all other stars and planets."

She learned, in her meditation, to experience that connectedness, that relationship with all life around her. "It is only in relationship to all other life," she was taught, "that we ourselves exist. Lao Tzu says we can know beauty only because of ugliness, can experience good only because of evil. Reality does not exist in a vacuum but only in relationship to all other forms of reality, including ourselves."

She learned to go deep within herself and work with her elemental forces in order to produce the great medicine, so much more powerful and eternal than any she could ever hope to make in an alchemist's laboratory. She became an inner alchemist, an inner explorer, and she traversed the mountains and deserts of her inner landscape to find ever new places of wisdom and delight.

Her teachers spoke of Tao as "the Valley Spirit" and "the Primal Yin." They used the image of the valley to symbolize the creativity and fecundity of the Tao. "The Tao is like an empty vessel," they said; "it can be used but never emptied." They spoke of the natural superiority of women over men in the energetic sense. "Man is fire," she was taught, "while woman is water. Fire is bright and impressive but all too often burns out without attaining anything of real value. Water, while it may take longer to come to boil, remains so for a longer time and can attain great things."

Women, they believed, were naturally closer to Tao and thus had an easier time in self cultivation. Secret practices were passed down from woman to woman that enabled them to reach great heights of insight and power, touch the surface of Tao and, if they persisted, to finally, one day "attain Tao," at which time they would become an immortal.

Chen Hua was still not quite sure what "attaining Tao" really meant but she was content in the knowledge she had gained and she felt stronger and more centered and rooted with each year.

For a while she had had a consort, a young man from a far away village who had traveled here, like her, to escape from a life of drudgery and ignorance. Together they had practiced dual cultivation and had shared their energies, their potent fluids. They had danced with each other on the winds of delight and had brought each other to the brink of ecstasy and then over. She had absorbed his vital essence into her own body as he did hers. Together they created a spiral of energy that reverberated into the world around them and sometimes took on a life of its own.

She had also done practices to unite the yin and yang within her own body. She blended and melded her own internal energies, creating what was called the Golden Embryo, in which she gave birth to a new self. No longer was she the stubborn, ignorant girl who asked endless questions—she was now a mature and self realized woman, a sage.

Now she lived alone at the base of the mountain. She had left the community of Taoists a few years before, deciding that for the last bit of her journey it would be best to remain alone. Her years with her fellow students of the Way had been fruitful and satisfactory. Her consort had gone on to another mountain to study with a master herbalist. She missed him but felt his presence within her constantly. The experiences they had shared had bonded them forever. Even now she could feel his cool touch on her body.

Her practices were of such a deep and subtle nature that it was difficult to live in close quarters with others. She was practicing the refinement of her energy to such a level that she needed to be able to control her personal environment as much as possible and so had to leave the family of Taoists that she had spent her life with. Besides, too many pilgrims were now drawn to their once solitary community and their constant noise and equally constant questions had begun to irritate her. She smiled when she remembered the many questions of her youth but realized that, while she wanted to answer all the pilgrims' questions, it took her away from her own practice. She was too far into it now to be distracted.

So she lived alone in her small yet comfortable hut by the noisy little creek; it filled her dreams with the music of water, of the ever flowing, ever faithful power of the yin, the Primal Valley Spirit. She spent her days in meditation, alternating between still sitting and slow, simple movement. Each day brought her closer to what the ancients called "attaining Tao," when she as Chen Hua would cease to exist and her *hun* and *po* spirits would separate and return to the earth and the universe from where they came. Her immortality would be a complete emergence into the undifferentiated oneness called Tao. Then like a flower unfolding, she would open her petals to the sun and radiate the true colors and joy of life itself.

In the meantime she lived her life, simply and gracefully, and greeted each new day as a gift, a wonder and a lesson to be treasured and learned.

Chapter Sources

Hua-Ching Ni, *Harmony, the Art of Life*
Mantak Chia, *Taoist Secrets of Love*
Ellen M. Chen, *The Tao Te Ching*
Charles Humana and Wang Wu, *The Chinese Way of Love*
Thomas Cleary, *Immortal Sisters*
Douglas Wile, *The Chinese Sexual Yoga Classics*
Hu-Ching, Ni *The Book of Changes and the Unchanging Truth*

14

True Medicine

To cure an illness that has already (physically) manifested itself is like starting to dig a well after one is already thirsty, or forging one's weapons after the battle has already begun.
Neijing

The Chinese method is thus holistic, based on the idea that no single part can be understood except in its relation to the whole.
Ted J. Katpchuk

Taoist medicine has its origin in ancient Taoist philosophy which views a person as an energy system wherein body and mind are unified, each influencing and balancing the other.
Hua-Ching Ni

In his seminal work *Tao: The Watercourse Way*, Alan Watts gives us the perfect view of the Taoist universe. Interestingly, it comes from the Buddhist monk Fa-tsang (643 CE to 712 CE) of the Mahayanist Hua-yen School, who described the universe as a multi-dimensional network of jewels, each one containing the reflections of all the others, ad infinitum. Each jewel was a *shih*, or "thing-event" and his principle of *shih shih wu ai* ("between one thing-event and another is no obstruction") expounded the mutual interpenetration and interdependence of everything happening in the universe.

Yun-men, a Chan Buddhist master said, "Medicine and sickness mutually correspond. The whole universe is medicine. What is the self?" Or as Roshi Aikten, a contemporary Zen master put it, "You and I come forth as possibilities of essential nature, alone and independent as stars, yet reflecting and being reflected by all things."

Native American tribes of North America, as do the Chinese, understand that the universe is divided into polarities. In this way, all elements are paired and balance each other. These elements consist of primal qualities: male and female, night and day, sun and moon, moist

and dry, dark and light, even tree and stone. It is through the awareness and the experience of this interdependence and relationship that
the universe, and within it we humans remains in balance.

Hippocrates, that ancient Greek to whom most Western physicians
owe historic allegiance, stressed the curative power of nature. He divided diseases, food and drugs, and times of the year into categories
of hot and cold, moist and dry, thereby regulating the human organ-
ism to its outer environment of geography, climate, season, weather
and diet.

What Is Medicine?

*Chinese medicine...is concerned with changes of state, dynamic and psy-
chic factors, function rather than substance.*
Manfred Porkert

The word medicine comes from the Latin *medicina*, which derives
from an ancient Indo-European root that also means remedy, meditate, and measure. Most people in our Western culture take medicine
to mean drugs of one sort or another. Indeed, the emphasis on drugs to
treat even minor problems has reached enormous proportions. The fact
that these drugs are often extremely potent, synthesized materials with
serious and often toxic side effects seems to matter little to the modern
healing profession.

In 1966 the American College of Physicians reported that about 5
percent of all hospital admissions were for iatrogenic diseases (diseases caused by adverse reactions to treatment). A more recent study
shows that 18 to 30 percent of all hospitalized patients experience some
adverse reaction to treatment, and that one seventh of all hospital days
are devoted to care of toxic reactions with the yearly cost to the patients of three billion dollars! Further, a 1981 report in the *New England
Journal of Medicine* said that 2 percent of cases of iatrogenic illnesses
contribute to the death of a patient. If that is correct, it means that about
700,000 people a year in the United States alone are affected, or one
third of the overall mortality rate.

These are frightening figures. Our culture has come a long way
from Paracelsus' statement, "The physician must cure the disease the
way it wants to be cured, not in the way he wants to cure it." The
medical system of this country and the American Medical Association
have become big business, and while many of its members are without
a doubt intelligent, caring and highly skilled doctors, an overall reliance on technological manipulations of the patient has developed, with

the cost of this care also rising ever upward.

The point is not to denigrate Western medicine, however. Many of the discoveries and implementations of modern science have offered much relief to the world of ill health. But one of the major factors of ill health in modern society is the numerous and often low key, but highly irritating, chronic diseases that so many of us live with. They account for vast amounts of medical problems. They often either go untreated or are treated for years with an arsenal of ever changing drugs (and ever changing side effects), all too frequently to no avail—and they cost us in depression, anxiety, time and money. It is just these kinds of imbalances—of not feeling quite right, that Chinese medicine is so good at alleviating.

As we become ever more cut off from our roots, further removed from our sense of connection—to the rest of the human race, our environment, and to the understanding of the interrelatedness of the universe itself—the phenomenon of chronic disease will become more and more prevalent. Not to mention the fact that chronic problems have a way of eventually becoming acute ones.

Chinese medicine is historically attuned to this kind of problem. In terms of preventative medicine, Chinese medicine really shines. Although it can be wonderfully effective in treating acute and traumatic conditions, it has much to offer in the way of relief from the numerous and exhaustive chronic imbalances brought on by our modern, stressed out, environmentally polluted, junk food eating society.

Modern men and women are solitary, lonely, cut off beings in much of the Western world. "Modern man is solitary," said Carl Jung, " and he is so of necessity and at all times, for every step toward a fuller consciousness of the present further removes him from his original participation with the mass of men—submersion in a common unconsciousness." In his book *Modern Man In Search Of A Soul*, Jung states that many of the psychiatric or mental problems are actually *spiritual* problems. Humankind as a whole, it would seem, is out of synch with its own nature, not to mention that of the nature surrounding it.

What we need is a system of medicine that considers the *whole* man and woman—their emotional, mental, spiritual as well as physical body. "The clinical gaze of oriental medicine," says Ted Kaptchuk, "recognized the continuum and interaction of the psyche and soma. The methodology has always taken into account the psychosomatic truth that psychological and physiological processes are interactive and have a shared clinical significance." In the mind/body (and in older traditions, spiritual) continuum is where Chinese medicine excels. To quote Jung again:

The psyche is not always and everywhere to be found on the inner side. It is to be found on the *outside* in whole races or periods of history which take no account of the psychic life as such.

We live in just such a time. Even Chinese medicine itself has forgotten or chosen to ignore an important part of its heritage. In all its various cultural and historical upheavals, some of the spiritual or purely mind/emotional qualities were dropped. Fortunately this aspect is being rediscovered and renewed and even elaborated upon at this time.

It's All Medicine

All phenomena of the world stimulate, tonify, subdue, or depress one's natural life force.
>   Neijing

Chinese medicine considers important certain aspects of the human body that are not significant to Western medicine.
>   Ted Kaptchuk

To traditional peoples, the concept of medicine means something very different than merely drugs. To Native Americans the word *medicine* means anything healing, and much more. It's also mystery, the sacred, the ineffable, the divine, the deeply personal. Each person has his or her own medicine. There is usually a strong injunction against interfering with another's medicine. Medicine is seen as anything which facilitates the movement of energy, good or bad, though the most frequent reference to medicine is as a healing or a spiritual agent.

Once, while attending an art opening for Kuis Lopez Kaocoatl, well known Aztec artist and *curandero*, (medicine man), I told him of my plans to study acupuncture. He remarked that his people used needles too. This surprised me, because I had never heard of such a thing. "It's all medicine," he said, shrugging.

"Medicine and sickness mutually correspond," says Yun-men. "The whole universe is medicine." It is by taking into account energy patterns, elemental imbalances, the use of crude forms of medicinal plants and minerals, the attention to the psyche *and* the soma aspects of disease and the principles of the unity of seeming opposites that the strength of Chinese medicine is to be felt and experienced.

To quote Andrew Weil:

Sickness and health are not simply physical states that the methods of science will eventually analyze completely and make understandable. They are rooted in the deepest and most mysterious strata of Being.

It is in this strata of being that Chinese medicine is firmly rooted and out of which it brings forth its attitudes and practices. It reminds us that we are interconnected in a very real and profound way to our inner as well as outer environment. It reminds us that it is our own energetic bodies that have the enormous and wonderful capacity for healing. It gives patients a sense of power, all too often stripped away by the overwhelmingly technological and compartmentalized attitudes of Western medicine. It gives us hope in our own capacity for self healing and self growth.

Yun-men asked the question, "What is the self?" The Lakota have a phrase, used after every prayer, that speaks to that question. "*Mitakuye Oyasin,*" they say, which roughly translates as "all my relations"; they take into account all living things in their prayer. It is the jeweled net of Fa-tsang, each jewel perfectly reflecting each other jewel, on and on into eternity. It is what is called true medicine by the old ones—medicine which takes into account all the old and all the new ways of being a human in this world. It speaks to *all* our parts, not just our bodies, not just our heads, not just our souls. It is a paradigm as rich and varied as any I have found and it works as well for Americans as Chinese. It is a profoundly human, in the highest sense, form of being and healing, sensitive to even the smallest change in the current of our self.

What is the self? Perhaps it is what we share with all other selves, the part of us we all know and share in our very humanness, the joyful, painful, sad and often lonely part, "alone and independent as stars, yet reflecting and being reflected by all things." It is the part of us that can heal, can affect another human (or animal or plant) in such a way that by our touch and attention, change can happen, healing can happen, wholeness can happen. It is just that part that Chinese medicine addresses, works in, and draws its greatest strength from.

Chinese Medicine

Taoists do not study disease; they study life and health and how to maintain them.
Stephen T. Chang

The Chinese system is not less logical than the Western, just less analytical.
Ted J. Kaptchuk

Chinese medicine treats today's medical problems as well as it did the afflictions besetting humankind thousands of years ago. It is a safe, non-invasive kind of medicine with virtually no side effects. Its curative powers are effective against mental and emotional ills as well as physical ailments.

The premise of Chinese medicine is simple. As part of a web of infinite dimension which connects everything in the universe, we humans are influenced by everything else in the web including the stars, the weather, the food we eat, the sounds we hear and all the things that touch us, including other humans. When we are in balance with all these things and, most importantly, within ourselves, we are healthy. But we are seldom in perfect balance—even with our immediate surroundings, much less within ourselves. And so, over centuries, the Chinese developed techniques to help us regain that balance, using gentle manipulation or massage, whole foods or medicinal herbs, and acupuncture.

As Maoshing Ni says in his excellent translation of the Chinese medicine classic, *Yellow Emperor's Classic of Medicine (Neijing)*:

> The student and practitioner of Chinese medicine will be amazed to find how little Chinese medicine has changed since the time the *Neijing* was written. Its natural therapies and preventive approaches are ever as effective and even more pertinent in today's drug-oriented medical climate. It offers a healthy and viable approach in the perception and treatment of illness. Especially in the battle against chronic, degenerative, infectious, and deficient medical conditions, Chinese medicine is promising as an effective alternative.

The *Neijing* is attributed to the great Huang Di, the Yellow Emperor, who reigned during the middle of the third millennium BCE. He has attained mythical status among the Chinese and is credited with the origin of Chinese medicine as well as dual cultivation. Its teachings are still used by Chinese doctors today and are as relevant as they were thousands of years ago. It advocates a life lived in accord with nature and the seasonal changes, both without and within the human body. As Maoshing Ni says:

> Health and well-being can be achieved only by remaining centered in spirit, guarding against the squandering of energy, promoting the constant flow of qi and blood, maintaining harmonious balance of yin and yang, adapting to the changing seasonal and yearly macrocosmic influences, and nourishing one's self preventively. This is the way to a long and happy life.

Most people in the West think of Chinese medicine as merely acupuncture, but it is much more than that. Classical Chinese medicine once contained eight sections including acupuncture, massage, feng shui (geomancy), qigong, meditation, and astrology. There were many different schools of Chinese medicine, some of which included the use of talismans (the writing of certain mystical symbols on paper, which were then burned and the ashes mixed with water and drunk), invocations, spirit communication, and the use of qigong to administer healing energy either directly into the body of the patient or into other substances such as water which was then swallowed by the patient.

The Three Treasures

The three treasures, also known as the three fundamental substances, are *jing, qi,* and *shen.* According to Chinese medicine, they are the substances which operate the human body.

Qi

Qi can be thought of as "basic life force," energy, prana, breath or simply vital energy. Ted Kaptchuk calls it "matter on the verge of becoming energy or energy on the point of materializing." In some ways, it is the very stuff of life. It is what animates us, what gives us life. It warms us, keeps our organs in their places, and directs all our movements.

There are different kinds of qi with different jobs to do. There is protective qi, or *wei qi.* It lies like an invisible electrical shield between the skin and the muscles. Its job is to keep out invading pathogens, or "outside evils." When our wei qi is low, our resistance to colds, flus and more serious viral invasions is weakened.

Another kind of qi is the organ qi. It is responsible for maintaining the strength and integrity of each organ in our bodies. When this kind of qi is weakened, our organ functions suffer and we are likely to have trouble breathing, digesting our food or sleeping. We may also suffer from a general feeling of fatigue.

Yet another kind of qi is meridian qi, which travels the pathways (called meridians or channels) throughout our bodies, linking organs to each other and to organ systems, and helping the blood move and stay within its channels. Meridian qi is what acupuncturists tap into when they insert their needles.

Herbalists also work with the qi in our bodies. They "tonify" or balance it, building it up where it is weak, draining off any excess and dispersing it when it becomes "stuck." Spiritual or energetic exercises or practices such as qigong can help us enhance and build up our stores of vital qi.

We get qi from the air we breathe and from the food we eat, which is why nutrition plays such a big part in the maintenance of good health. Certain foods contain different qualities of qi. Whole, unprocessed, fresh and organic foods contain an abundance of strong, vital qi, which is passed along to us when we eat it. On the other hand, refined, over-processed and adulterated foods contain little qi.

Clearly, good eating habits are extremely important in maintaining or building good health. The ancient Taoists, while very spiritual, were also very practical, and they believed strongly that by feeding their bodies the right foods, providing appropriate exercise and breathing correctly, they were taking the best possible care of a sacred gift—the gift of life itself.

Qi may also be thought of as electricity. It can't be seen, yet it most certainly can be felt. You can even think of the meridian system in the human body as an electrical system complete with junctures, fuse boxes and miles of wiring, all connecting in one great multi-level energy circuit.

Primal qi can also be thought of as the animating, creative force of the universe. In Hua-Ching Ni's book, *The Book of Changes and the Unchanging Truth*, primal qi is described as follows:

How can the universe be alive? Because it is the continual transformation of primal chi, the pivotal energy and living soul of the universe. Primal chi functions as the subtle connection of the universe in the same way that the nervous system functions in the human body. It extends itself primordially as the self-nature of the universe.

And:

By understanding that all things in the universe are just different expressions of chi, one can see why the sages have always said, "All things are one, and the one is all things." Without the outreach and withdrawal, the giving and returning of chi, the transformation of all things would be impossible.

All Taoist practices, spiritual or health oriented, work with qi. Even spirituality is seen as a form of qi or energy, but in the physical realm qi plays a major role in our day to day health issues. That is why Chinese medicine is so concerned with balancing, tonifying and freeing up areas of "stuck" qi in the body.

Jing

Jing, sometimes referred to as prenatal qi, is a combination of the qi of both our parents which we receive at conception, and it governs our constitutions. Conception at a time when one or both parents are under the influence of alcohol, or when they are seriously unhealthy, or even when they are emotionally overwrought can lead to poor jing, which in turn produces a weak constitution. It also regulates our hormonal and reproductive systems, controls our growth throughout life, and regulates our central nervous system, including the brain, spinal cord and bone marrow. It is said that it takes seven mouthfuls of food to make one drop of blood. It then takes seven drops of blood to make one drop of jing, which is why it is called "essence" and considered extremely precious.

We all have a finite amount of jing, or essence, which can either be squandered or preserved. We've all seen people with hearty constitutions succumb in middle age to heart attacks, diabetes or cancer because they abused their bodies for years. On the other hand, those born with weak constitutions can overcome their afflictions and live long, productive lives if they protect this treasure rather than burn themselves out needlessly.

Jing is said to be stored in the kidneys, the repositories of sexual and reproductive energy. The aging process has much to do with using up our jing (ideally little by little) as we go through life. Unfortunately men lose small amounts of jing with each ejaculation, which is why they tend to be outlived by their female partners.

Shen

The last treasure is the shen or spirit. It may also be called consciousness, that which makes us human. It gives our lives meaning and links us with our divine source. The shen is said to reside in the heart, though it is visible to practitioners in a patient's eyes (just as in the old adage that "the eyes are the mirror of the soul"). A traditional Chinese physician can tell the seriousness of a condition by looking into the patient's eyes. Bright or clear eyes indicate that the shen or spirit is strong; then the chances of recovery are good. Clouded, glazed or unfocused eyes indicate a more doubtful prognosis.

The shen is also the seat of the mind. Cognitive thinking, short-term memory and the ability to reason are all qualities of the shen. It too is formed at conception, but is replenished continually thereafter.

The Organs

When speaking of organs in Chinese medical tradition, it is important to understand that we are not speaking of the actual physical organ but rather of the energetic qualities attributed to it.They are looked at as function rather than form. Therefore, when a traditional Chinese physician says that you have weak kidneys, it doesn't mean you're a candidate for dialysis! It simply means the energetic quality of your kidneys is weak, thereby adversely affecting the kidneys' paired or related organs such as the adrenal glands.

Remember that in Taoist thought the human body is a microcosm of the entire universe. Our organs, also called heavenly orbs or celestial spheres, are analogous to, even directly related to, the heavenly bodies of the solar system. They are regarded as living, pulsing, vibrating centers of energy within our bodies. This link with the heavenly bodies in space explains why astrology played such a major role in traditional Chinese thought.

The organs are divided into two categories: the *zang* or yin organs and the *fu* or yang organs. The zang organs are the solid organs, and they are involved with pure substances and refining processes. They are considered the most important. The fu organs involve the gross transformation of substances, and each is paired with a supporting zang organ. Zang organs are the spleen, which is paired with the stomach; the liver, paired with the gall bladder; the kidneys, paired with the urinary bladder; the heart, paired with the small intestine; the lungs, paired with the large intestine. An interesting fu organ is the triple warmer, which is concerned with metabolism and the proper and smooth functioning of and communication among the three areas of the body—upper, middle and lower. The triple warmer is paired with the pericardium, which is thought to be the protector of the heart.

Each organ, besides having an energetic or medical aspect in the body, also carries a particular emotional resonance as well as relationships with a particular time of the year, color, element and taste or flavor, among other things.

Kidneys

In Chinese medicine, the kidneys function together with the adrenal glands. They govern urinary function and the sexual and reproductive organs, and they also house the *jing* which is responsible for the growth and development of the body. They are the source of the body's resistance and endurance, of physical, emotional and spiritual tenacity. They are the seat of will power and are generally regarded as the "batteries" of the body.

One curious role the kidneys play is called "grasping the qi." When we inhale, the kidneys exert a grasping or pulling effect on the air, drawing it down into our lungs. For this reason, many asthmatics, especially those with trouble inhaling, will receive acupuncture treatment for the kidneys as well as the lungs.

The kidneys are said to open into the ears. In other words, kidney problems will often manifest in the ears, as with deafness, ringing, or inner ear problems such as dizziness. Other complaints of deficient kidney qi include insomnia and, because of its special relationship with the heart, mental confusion. Lower back pain may be experienced because that is where the kidneys are located in the body.

The kidneys are a source of much of the body's day to day energy. They can be thought of as the pilot light under the furnace. If the flame is too low, the entire heating system will perform inadequately. Chronic fatigue conditions are generally a sign of weak kidneys.

The element associated with the kidneys is water, the emotion is fear (kidney problems also contribute to excessive fear or anxiety), the color is blue-black, the season is winter and the flavor, salty.

Spleen

When the Chinese refer to the spleen, they include the stomach by definition, since the two are paired in the process of digestion. A weak spleen means weak digestion and thus a poor absorption of qi from our nutritional intake. The spleen is in charge of transforming food into qi, keeping the blood in the vessels and holding the other organs in place. Spleen problems could include abdominal distention, blood in the stool or urine, and general digestive disorders.

The element associated with the spleen is earth, its color is yellow, its season is harvest time and its flavor, sweet. The emotional tone often associated with the spleen is empathy, though in its negative sense it becomes worry or self-absorption. The tendency to go over and over a problem searching for an elusive solution is regarded as a sign of spleen weakness.

Liver

Besides filtering toxins, the liver is the storehouse of the blood in that it regulates the amount of blood in the vessels and stores a large amount of blood at night. It also regulates movement within the body such as the flow of qi, blood, hormones, lymph and even emotions, thus preventing blockage within the system.

The liver is said to open into the eyes; many eye problems such as floating spots, red, dry or painful eyes, as well as problems focusing, are often treated by paying attention to the liver.

Anger is the emotion associated with the liver. Often, someone will be said to have "constrained liver qi," which means the person's liver is tight and so are his/her emotions. Unexpressed anger injures the liver, as does alcohol, which heats it up. The red eyes and belligerence of some alcoholics is attributed to a heated liver.

The element of the liver is wood, the season is spring, the color is green and the flavor, sour.

Lungs

The lungs dominate the qi and respiration, as well as regulate water passages. This means they send body fluids to the skin, to the kidneys and bladder, to the muscles and throughout the rest of the body. Lung imbalances could result in respiratory problems, as well as edema (water retention) and swelling in the face or upper body, or excessive sweating. Since the lungs are connected to the skin, lung dysfunction could also lead to skin problems.

The positive emotion associated with the lungs is courage, while the negative emotion is grief. As with the liver, unexpressed or excess grief can injure the lungs.

The element associated with the lungs is metal, the season is autumn, the color is white and the flavor, spicy.

Heart

As mentioned previously, the heart houses the shen, or spirit. It also controls blood circulation and dominates the blood vessels. Except for cardiac irregularity, problems with the heart tend to be either shen disturbances such as mental illness, memory loss, insomnia, unclear thinking or, since it opens onto the tongue, it may manifest as stuttering or other speech difficulties.

The positive emotion associated with the heart is joy, while the negative emotion is hysteria. The Taoists even say that too much joy can injure the heart. The element of the heart is fire, the color is red, the season is summer and the flavor, bitter.

Again it is important to remember that we are speaking of something quite other than the Western anatomical organ. Rather, we are speaking of two somewhat separate functions—a physical form as well as an energetic form. Some even call it the spiritual form, as in the following quote from Cheng Man-Ching:

> The heart is not the lump of flesh known as the heart, but the spiritual heart. The spiritual heart and the heart of flesh were not originally two but also not one. That is to say, the reason why the heart, which is flesh, is able to function and more subtly than anything else is because of the spiritual heart.

Diagnosis and Treatment
Eight-Condition Diagnosis

In this country, a visit to most practitioners of Chinese medicine begins with what is called "eight condition diagnosis" wherein the problem or complaint of the patient will usually be assigned to one or more of eight different categories. The practitioner is concerned with whether the problem is of a yin or yang nature and whether it is due to a deficiency or an excess, an exterior or interior condition, or a condition of hot or cold.

The Chinese do not think only in terms of specific diseases, each with its own particular etiology. They consider problems to be disharmonies adversely affecting the proper balances of the body. This enables them to look at each patient as an individual with an individual set of needs. Chinese medicine is the original "holistic" medicine, and has been for thousands of years!

As Ted J. Kaptchuk tells us:

> Western medicine is concerned mainly with isolatable disease categories or agents of disease, which it zeroes in on, isolates, and tries to change, control or destroy. The Western physician starts with a symptom, then searches for the

underlying mechanism—a precise *cause* for a specific *disease*.

On the other hand, says Kaptchuk, what the Chinese see as patterns of disharmony "are different from diseases because they cannot be isolated from the patient in whom they occur."

The Chinese believe that disease or disharmony can be caused either by an internal imbalance or by an external condition such as an invading pathogen—the "evil wind" or "external pernicious influence" which Western doctors would describe as a bacterial or viral infection. An external invasion may be "damp or dry" or "cold or hot." We've all experienced a sudden chill accompanied by muscular aches and maybe even a headache. On the other hand, a sudden onset may be accompanied by fever or a sore throat. A Western doctor would call both conditions "colds" or "flu" and treat them similarly. A Chinese practitioner would treat them differently, either as a hot or cold invasion.

Internal imbalances can also cause disease. Poor nutrition, weak constitution, overwork, stress, drug or alcohol use, even unbalanced emotions can cause internal disharmony, and each must be dealt with accordingly.

Sometimes our qi, or the qi of an individual organ, can become depleted due to stress and disease. A low voice, weak movements, shallow breathing and a pale or white face are all signs of qi deficiency. In this case herbs, acupuncture to stimulate various meridians, or a combination of both would be used to tonify or build up the energy in that part of the body and its connecting organs.

Sometimes disharmony is of an excessive nature, indicating that there is too much energy in certain areas. A red face, loud voice, forceful or abrupt movements and heavy breathing are all signs of excess. Sometimes headaches are caused by an excess of energy or heat in the head. The treatment then is to draw the excess off into another section of the system, or perhaps to disperse it so that its intensity is decreased. Once again, herbs, acupuncture, or both can be used.

Symptoms the Chinese refer to as cold include a feeling of coldness and a desire for warmth, pain that is reduced by heat, watery stools and clear or white secretions. Heat symptoms, on the other hand, include a red face and eyes, fever, thirst, a feeling of hot and an aversion to cold, and thick or yellowish secretions.

It is interesting to note that, contrary to Western diagnosis, if the patient feels hot whether or not s/he has a fever, it is considered a heat condition and treated just as if fever were present.

All disharmonies can be said to be of a yin or yang nature, yet yin and yang ailments are still but two of the eight conditions. Yin is considered to be an internal, nourishing type of energy relating to cold or coolness and having to do with both the blood (as in whether it's flowing properly through the vessels, and at what strength) and rest, or inactivity. Yang is considered an external, protective type of energy having to do with heat or warmth, related to yin and concerned with movement or activity.

As previously mentioned, yin/yang theory concerns itself with relative balance. The Chinese do not believe in absolutes; rather, they believe reality to be flexible, ever changing, and defined by its relation to other aspects of itself. As the *Tao Te Ching* says, good is only seen as good in relation to evil. Even in medical practice, a warm condition will be judged in relation to the balance of warm and cool energies in the body. Different times of the year, different diets, even different body types will all come to bear on the diagnosis. Then, if the body is being harmed by too much heat, cooling herbs will be administered.

The main idea is to help the body achieve homeostasis, or internal harmony. Then the body's own innate intelligence can correct the problem. It is a way of working from the bottom up to get to the root of our problems, which may not be apparent from the symptoms. After all, we are exposed to countless viruses and bacteria every day, in addition to those which already live in our bodies. Why does one person succumb when his neighbor does not?

There are, of course, many factors involved. Constitutional makeup, weak areas of the body, stress levels and many other variables can influence how and when we get sick. The key is to balance our weaknesses, our strengths, our stress and even our attitudes about health and sickness. By using yin and yang, or the relative nature of each, we can begin to develop a helpful perspective on our situation.

As mentioned earlier, few people's problems fit neatly into one or more categories. Instead, these problems often include aspects of all eight, plus an almost infinite number of subcategories. Rarely is there only one thing going on at a time, but each person's internal landscape is a combination of various influences and conditions. That's the challenge, and the art, of Chinese medicine. Each person is regarded as an individual with his or her own particular set of influences and disharmonies.

Rarely are two people treated exactly the same way, even when they have the same Western-diagnosed disease etiology. For example, if a Western physician diagnosed six people as having ulcers, it's likely that all six would be treated with the same medication and diet. A practitioner of Chinese medicine, however, recognizes that ulcers may be caused by any number of problems, and they are likely to interact differently with each individual's own unique emotional and physical makeup. Thus the treatment would be tailored to the precise needs of each individual patient.

The Quinary or Five Phases

The five phases or elements is another method of diagnosis and treatment. This somewhat complicated system of correspondences should not be thought of in terms of absolute forms, but rather as the "five quintessential processes" of fire, earth, metal, water and wood. As in much of Chinese medicine and philosophy, these terms are relative and apt to shift in and out of each other, depending on their use. According to this system, all major organs are assigned to one of the specific elements, along with a specific color, taste, emotion, and so forth.

The phrase *wu hsing* is often translated as "five elements" but that is misleading. Wu hsing means literally "five to go" and is concerned primarily with the ever-shifting primal qualities that exist in nature, both within and without. In constitutional Chinese medicine individuals are studied very closely to determine which of the elements predominate in that individual's make-up, much like the Indian system of medicine called Ayurveda. We all have both strengths and weaknesses and these can change as we go through our life. But by paying close attention to the balance or imbalance of the five phases of our system we can better attain that hoped-for state of balance and harmony that all Taoists aspire to.

The five phases work in two major cycles of relationship: the *shen*, or promotion cycle, and the *ko*, or control cycle. These particular cycles may be used in many different ways in health care and treatment.

The promotion or growth cycle starts with fire as the mother of earth. Earth, in turn, is the mother of metal. Metal is the mother of water. Water is the mother of wood, and wood is the mother of fire. An easy way to remember this cycle is that fire makes ashes which produce earth; from earth we take metal; metal can hold or be a container for water; water nourishes wood or new growth; and wood feeds fire.

The shen cycle is also called the mother/child relationship, because one grows out of the other, and both influences and is influenced by the other. This is why, in treating weakness in a "child organ," a practitioner may transfer energy from the "mother organ," or actually treat the mother organ in order to benefit the child. As the analogy goes, if a nursing baby is irritable and weak, look to the mother. If she is unhealthy and gives poor milk, no amount of treating the child will help. One must treat the mother and improve her health so that she gives an abundance of good, nourishing milk, and then the child will prosper.

Another example of how this works is the case of headache and dizziness. This is usually related to the liver, or wood element, being out of harmony or deficient. But in some cases, the cause of the difficulty is the water element, or kidneys. If the kidneys fail to properly nourish the wood, the liver energy will rise up and enter the head. But by tonifying the kidneys, or water element, the liver can be calmed, and the headache or dizziness will disappear. In this case, the mother has been strengthened in order to treat the child.

Likewise a chronic cough, although associated with the lungs or metal element, may actually be caused by a weakness in the spleen, or the earth element which creates metal. In this case, simply treating the lungs may actually make the condition worse. But tonifying the mother organ, the spleen, will fortify its child, the lungs.

The ko, or control cycle, works a little differently. In this cycle, fire controls metal, metal controls wood, wood controls earth, earth controls water and water controls fire. To understand these relationships, consider that fire, if hot enough, can melt metal; metal, forged into an ax or saw, will cut wood; wood, fashioned into tools, can penetrate the earth; earth can be built into a dam to hold back water; and, of course, water will extinguish fire.

In this cycle, care is given to avoid a situation where one organ interferes with another, as when "liver invades spleen" or wood "insults" earth. Here, we would have digestive disturbances as well as diarrhea and distended abdomen. In this case, the liver energy needs to be calmed and the spleen energy fortified.

In other words, we must always take the energy from where there is too much to where there is too little. And a practitioner must always work in the correct direction of the energy flow. It has been said that if the child is hungry, it should be put to the breast; but if the mother is hungry, do not give her the child to eat! Of course, an internal deficiency may also be treated by bringing energy into the body from the outside via herbs or other sources of nutrition.

In Chinese medicine, it is believed that colors affect us at a profound level. In fact, practitioners can get a good idea of the status of our internal organs by asking which colors a patient prefers and avoids. You have probably had the experience of feeling totally enraptured by a certain color, only to find yourself feeling a complete aversion to it later. This is your bodily intelligence system filing a report. To take advantage of it, keep a mental log of which colors stimulate or calm you, and which colors actually set off internal alarms.

Colors also play a role in diagnosis when the practitioner looks for changes in the patient's natural coloring. The greenish tinge of a sick person's face is a familiar sight, but colors ranging from yellow to black are also clear indicators of the patient's internal condition.

Tastes, too, can tell you a lot about what your organs are doing. The *Ling Shu*, part of the *Neijing* says:

Each of the five tastes moves to what it likes. If the taste of the nourishment is sour, it moves first to the liver; if bitter, it moves to the heart; if sweet, it moves first to the spleen; if hot, it moves first to the lungs; if salty, it moves first to the kidneys.

Thus, preferences or even cravings can be evidence of the condition of the bodily system. The Chinese even believe that too much of a certain flavor will damage the related organ and could send the entire system out of balance.

As always, the aim of Chinese medicine is to effect a balance, not only of yin and yang, but of all phases of the human being: the physical, emotional, mental as well as the spiritual aspects of human life. Keeping all these in perspective and in balance, we may live long and healthy lives.

Herbs

Herbs give everlasting strength, whereas regular foods give only temporary strength.

Stephen T. Chang

The Taoist sages were very adept at observing nature, and they learned the use of many herbs by watching what animals ate when they were injured or sick. It was over 5,000 years ago that the great emperor Shen Nong discovered the properties of a great many herbs by ingesting them himself—a brave though potentially fatal way of going about it!

Originally, herbs were thought of as food—highly nutritious, beneficial food. The ancient Chinese formulae, or recipes, spoke of herbal "soups" rather than teas. Herbs were eaten as part of the daily meal, cooked into soups or broths, or eaten as salads. There were, of course, purely medicinal herbs, but for the most part, herbs were used as a means of strengthening or maintaining the integrity of the body.

The Chinese also use a great many substances in their pharmacopoeia, some of which may be surprising. A compendium by the famous physician Li Shi-zhen (published in 1596) includes 1,892 entries. Of these, 1,173 are botanical ingredients, 444 are zoological or animal-derived, and 275 are derived from minerals. The most recently published pharmacopoeia lists 5,767 entries! Over thousands of years of observation, exploration and experimentation, the Chinese herbalists were able to find specific uses for an incredible range of substances, from the lovely chrysanthemum flower to the lowly earthworm!

Chinese medicine's greatest strength is in preventing disease or disharmony. In ancient times, you paid your physician to keep you well. If he didn't do his job properly and you became ill, he would provide you with curative treatment at no charge (providing, of course, that you had been following his instructions properly). How different from today's attitude toward health care! In this modern age, we only think of seeing a doctor or other healer after we become sick, when it's much harder to treat the disorder.

Chinese herbal theory is very different from its Western counterpart in that it does not concern itself so much with the biochemical properties of the herb. Rather, it thinks in terms of energetic properties. Will the herb bring about a cooling influence or a warming one? Will it draw energy in or dispel it? Will it expand energy or condense it? The synergistic effects of the herbs, or how they interact with other herbs in a formula, are also a consideration. Chinese herbal formulae are a combination of herbs working together to bring about harmony within the whole system. Many have been used for thousands of years.

Today, one can get raw herbs from an herb store or a qualified practitioner. You may also get what are called patent medicines, which are herbal extracts made into small pills. Granulated or other forms of concentrated herbs may also be used. Whatever the form, Chinese herbs are a safe, effective part of a 5,000-year tradition of study and treatment.

Another way herbs can be used is for spiritual cultivation, called *lian dan shu* or the art of alchemy. In this way herbs are used to open spiritual centers in the body, rid the body of negative or dark energies and dissolve emotional congestion. Maoshing Ni says that the "basic goals of any lian dan discipline or cultivation are ultimately, to minimize within oneself the negative, turbid and pathological energies and to accumulate and refine the positive, creative and light energies."

In ancient days some Taoist practitioners used various herbal substances to concoct an "immortality pill" thought to confer immortality on anyone who swallowed it. Many strong, often poisonous substances were used, sometimes to disastrous effects. Many Chinese emperors, including the first emperor Shih Huang Di, were said to have died from ingesting such pills.

The truth was that the real practitioners of lian dan shu spoke of minerals such as gold, silver, jade and mercury as methods of an internal alchemical process and never meant for them to be consumed.

As Maoshing Ni tells us:

The flamboyant and secretive nature of alchemy employing exotic minerals aroused wide attention and imagination from the public while the knowledge and use of botanical supplements were kept quietly in the grasp of a few select Taoist lineages.

The metaphor of lian dan involves taking raw material and refining it in an alchemical synthesis. This makes the ultimate outcome a pure, enhanced and powerful manifestation which increases the quality and span of one's life at minimum. At optimum, the physical boundaries are transcended and the enjoyment of absolute spiritual immortality is attained.

Chinese herbs are divided into three major categories: toxic herbs, which are extremely potent herbs used for life saving situations only; medicinal herbs, which are used for specific health problems; and food herbs, which are for everyday use as part of high quality nutrition. Medicinal herbs should only be used under care of a qualified practitioner but food herbal formulas are becoming more common and can be eaten safely as part of one's general nutrition.

Acupuncture

The practice of acupuncture is based on the meridian theory in which qi, or vital energy, is believed to travel through precise pathways or meridians. There are twelve major meridians, each connected to a particular organ, plus eight special or "extra" meridians. There are also innumerable smaller meridians throughout the body.

The meridians connect the organs to each other and connect the interior of the body to the exterior. They actually form a sort of grid or road map of the entire bodily system. Acupuncture is the practice of placing extremely thin needles at special junctures or "points" along these meridians in order to affect the energy and balance of the body. Needling is said to "reduce what is excessive, increase what is deficient, warm what is cold, cool what is hot, circulate what is stagnant, move what is congealed, stabilize what is reckless, raise what is falling and lower what is rising."

There are about 365 points on the body (not including the "special" or "extra" points or those which are part of the modern auricular or ear systems), although most practitioners only use about 150. The acupuncturist must be extremely sensitive and observant in determining exactly which of these points to use, and how. It is a very demanding yet very delicate art, one which can bring about sublime and at times dramatic changes in one's energy level, healing capacity and even one's outlook on life.

One of the most dramatic roles of acupuncture, and probably the most familiar to Westerners, is its use as anesthesia or analgesia. All sorts of major surgical procedures are done today in China with little or no anesthesia other than acupuncture. During a highly publicized trip to China in the early 1970s, one member of President Nixon's party was stricken with appendicitis. His appendectomy was performed using acupuncture instead of traditional Western anesthesia, and he was soon telling everyone back home about his amazing experience. This accidental publicity helped to open many doors for the now commonly accepted use of acupuncture in the United States.

Various theories attempt to explain how acupuncture works as anesthesia. One idea is that the needles block the pain impulse as it moves through the central nervous system and prevent it from reaching the brain. Another is that the needles stimulate the release of endorphins, our bodies' own natural pain killers.

Acupuncture is also used in the Western world to treat addictions. Primarily ear points are used to reduce the cravings for alcohol, drugs and cigarettes. Many people also report far fewer withdrawal symptoms when they use acupuncture in their efforts to free themselves of chemical dependency, partly because the detoxifying treatment strengthens the organ system in order to support the addict's ability to cope with stress.

It is clear that acupuncture has many uses in today's world. It is a simple form of treatment which has neither side effects nor risk of addiction. And it works as well in veterinary use as it does on humans.

A Visit to the Practitioner

A visit to a practitioner of Chinese medicine will be a bit different from an appointment with a Western physician. The practitioner may begin by asking a lot of questions, some of them seemingly quite strange. Do you feel hot or cold? Do you have any pain? How many times do you get up at night to urinate? Are you thirsty? Do you crave hot drinks or cold ones? How are your bowel movements? How is your sleep? Do you have headaches or dizziness? If you are a woman, how is your menstrual cycle? Is it regular? Is the flow thick or thin? If you are having any discharge, what color is it and is there any odor?

All the while the practitioner is talking with you, s/he will also be observing your facial color, the manner in which you are breathing, the tone and volume of your voice, the way you move. Even the way you sit on your chair can tell a practitioner of Chinese medicine a lot about your internal condition.

The practitioner may then look closely at your tongue, observing its color, its size and the presence of any coating or moss, including its texture and color. The tongue is a mirror of the internal organs. Over the millennia, tongue diagnosis has evolved into a fine art. Then, perhaps strangest of all, the practitioner will feel the pulses along the wrists of both your arms. Those who are trained in Chinese medicine can learn a great deal from palpating three adjacent areas along the medial artery of the wrist. Feeling for strength, rate of pulsation and the depth of each pulse, they can ascertain the health and integrity of all the major organs. A master can even detect a history of childhood illnesses and the probability of future problems, all from feeling the wrist!

Even the diagnosis is apt to sound strange. "Deficient kidney yin," "deficient blood," "internal wind," "liver invading spleen." These are but a few of the exotic sounding diagnoses you may hear.

Now comes the treatment. It may take the form of acupuncture, tui na massage, moxibustion (burning herbs over the points, inducing a healing warmth), or herbs, or perhaps a combination of all or some of the above.

Acupuncture needles are quite thin—nothing like hypodermic needles. They are usually inserted quite shallowly so that they do not hurt at all. Occasionally, there will be a slight prick as the needle enters, but the discomfort disappears as soon as the insertion is complete. Of course, tender areas such as the toes or the face may be more sensitive. But even so, acupuncture is not nearly as painful as an injection or "shot."

The acupuncturist is looking for a tingling sensation or a dull, achey feeling. This is called "obtaining the qi." The sensation is caused by the qi itself as it moves along its pathway. The sensation is not painful and in fact is considered a positive sign.

A treatment may consist of only a few needles, or many. It all depends on the problem the acupuncturist needs to treat. The needles are often left in for ten to twenty minutes, though in sensitive or weak patients they may be left in for only a few brief moments.

Acupuncture, like herbal therapy, usually takes awhile to bring results, although dramatic results have sometimes been produced in one or two acupuncture treatments or a week or two of herbs. Most practitioners have had the experience of seeing a patient arrive for treatment on crutches, only to leave without them! But generally Chinese medicine takes time because it deals with regeneration rather than substitution. Chinese medicine uses the body's own resources to do the healing work. In nutritional or herbal therapy, the body is fed highly nutritious and balancing herbal foods so that it will come into balance on its own.

People rarely get sick in a day. By the time afflictions manifest themselves with serious or even just uncomfortable symptoms, they will have been building for some time. Therefore, it will take time to reroute the energy or build up the reserves and re-balance the internal harmony of the system. Chinese medicine generally works from the bottom up, except in certain acute situations. That means it is working to create a strong foundation on which to build strong health.

Nowadays in China qigong is used as often as acupuncture, if not more so, to treat people. In the next chapter we will explore this fascinating subject.

J.R. Worsley, a founder of his own school of acupuncture in Britain has written:

This system of medicine is based on the most solid foundation of any system of medicine in the world. It is wholly based on natural laws. Man cannot pollute it; man cannot change it; man cannot improve upon it. Although it may be new in the Western world, one has to recognize that one-quarter of the world's population has been treated by this system of medicine, for over five thousand years. If it was not valid, then it would have died thousands of years ago.

Manfred Porkert tells us of Bian Que, a contemporary of Confucius, who was a famous doctor and author of the *Nanjing* (classic of difficult cases). He gives us the six varieties or indications of incurable disease, which I think clearly illustrate the unique approach of Chinese medicine:

1. Arrogance and capriciousness that exceed the bounds of reason.
2. Insufficient regard of the integrity of one's own person, together with an excessive regard for riches and treasures.
3. A propensity for improper foods and inappropriate clothing.
4. Disharmony between yin and yang, and the ensuing instability of the flow of active energy.
5. Total cachexia (wasting, loss of muscular strength), so that medications cannot be administered any longer.
6. Misplaced faith in the abilities of sorcerers, as opposed to physicians (whose treatments are based on rational principles).

How different from our modern attitude toward health, where we see ourselves as victims of outside invasions or mysterious inner growths!

In the end we are left with the image of the great jeweled net, each facet of each jewel reflecting off each of the others, creating a constantly shifting reality of balance and harmony. Chinese medicine, with its orientation of working with internal forces and how they balance with the outer can be a powerfu tool for healing and transformation.

True medicine comes in many forms, as I wrote in the following poem.

Eagle wing   •   Owl feather.
    Tiny round stones the ant people
    have brought up from the underworld.
Shell of the sea,
    Wood so old it's turned to stone.
Sweatlodge   •   Nightchant
    Ginseng man root.
Incense—cedar and sweetgrass,
    frankincense and myrrh.
Herbs from the mountains,
    Qi from someone who cares.
Golden needles   •   Burning moxa.

The true medicine being in what you
bring to it—not the object itself.

A song, treasured and sung alone
    in silence.
A gift of the heart,
    a touch, a smile, a caress.
Coyote magic—kick in the butt.
    A stone that spoke to me
A crystal that shone, so bright!
    A dream too real to be dreamt,
A gathering of souls,
 one heart, one mind,
Medicine for the sick.

It is said:
    True medicine heals
    from the inside out.

Chapter Sources

Manfred Porkert, *Chinese Medicine*
Ted. J. Kaptchuk, *The Web That Has No Weaver*
Alan Watts, *Tao: The Watercourse Way*
Robert Aitken, *The Mind of Clover*
Manfred Porkert, *Chinese Medicine*
Jane English & Gia-fu Feng, *Tao Te Ching*
Bruce Holbrook, *The Stone Monkey*
Andrew Weil, *Health and Healing*
Carl Jung, *Modern Man In Search of a Soul*
Maoshing Ni, *The Yellow Emperor's Classic of Medicine*
Stephen T. Chang, *The Great Tao*
Hua-Ching Ni, *The Book of Changes and the Unchanging Truth*
Hua-Ching Ni, *Tao: The Subtle Universal Law
    and the Integral Way of Life*
Hua-Ching Ni, *Power of Natural Healing*
Cheng Man Ching, *Master Cheng's Thirteen Chapters
    on T'ai-Chi Ch'uan*
Paul U. Unschuld, *Medicine in China: A History of Ideas*
Maoshing Ni, *interview in The Empty Vessel:
    A Journal of Contemporary Taoism*
J.R. Worsley, *Talking About Acupuncture in New York*

15

Organ Balancing Meditation

Sitting quietly, breathing gently and slowly, from the belly, eyes closed, seeing with the mind's eye.

Imagine a cloud of light hovering just above your head. It can be a billowy, fluffy cloud, or a sparkling cloud of energy, or whatever other form feels right to you. Feel it floating there, just above your head, for a moment or two. Then let it slowly sink down through the top of your head, through the *bai hui* point, to settle in your heart.

Here it becomes a bright, vibrant red. Red is the color of summer, when all of life is at its peak. It is a joyous, creative time, when the bright sun shines mightily down upon us all. Feel this season in your heart as the red cloud pulses slowly in your chest. The element is Fire, the fire of controlled passion and creativity.

The heart's job is to keep the blood moving freely throughout the body. It is also the home of the shen, or spirit. It is that which makes us human, that which gives us consciousness.

The negative emotion connected with the heart is hysteria. The positive, which we are emphasizing right now, is joy and creativity. So picture this vibrant red cloud lying lightly on your heart, filling it with joy and purpose, openness and creativity.

Sit and relax for a little bit and allow yourself to feel this deep within you. Remember, in Taoist practice, "qi follows yi," or energy goes with the mind. Wherever you put your attention is where the energy will go, positively or negatively. This is why it is important to always keep our thoughts positive and supportive so this will be the kind of energy we will not only attract, but create within ourselves.

Next we move down to the left side of our abdomen to our spleen/ stomach area. Here the cloud turns to a vibrant, earthy yellow. The spleen element is Earth, its season is harvest time or, as was observed in ancient times, the pause between seasons. It is the grounding force in our being.

The spleen helps our digestion, extracting the qi from what we eat. It also helps us digest our experiences. The negative emotion connected to the spleen is worry or self-absorption; the positive emotion is empathy.

Take a little time here and allow yourself to feel your empathy and connection to the earth and to all living things. Feel the groundedness of your being. Sink your roots deep within the earth; draw up the pure yin qi found there and let it fill you up, from the bottoms of your feet to the top of your head.

Now move the cloud up to your chest and into your lungs. When it reaches your lungs it turns bright white. It hovers there, within your lungs, filling them with vital, healing energy. The corresponding season is autumn, the time when growing things are beginning to close up shop for the long sleep of winter. The element is Metal or Gold (or what the Greeks referred to as Air).

The lungs rule the respiration, our ability to extract oxygen and other nutrients, as well as qi, from the air around us. And they govern our *wei* or protective qi, guarding us against outside evils or attacking forces like colds and flus. Picture then, your lungs becoming strong and healthy, expanding easily with each breath, sending out the protective qi to all parts of your body, each cell expanding and contracting as you breathe deeply through the belly.

The negative emotion connected with the lungs is grief. It is here we feel our sadness, our loss. And while we acknowledge the importance of connecting to that grief and not denying or suppressing it, at this time we would like to emphasize the positive emotions of courage and the ability to surrender deeply to each moment.

We picture and feel these attributes of courage and the ability to surrender as we see this bright white cloud of energy lying loosely upon our lungs.

Next we move to our lower back, to the kidneys. Here the cloud turns a deep blue/black, almost black. The element is Water, the season winter, the time when earth energy is dormant and deep. The kidney/adrenal area is the seat of our will. It also is the source of our day-to-day energy, the pilot light beneath our furnace.

Here we store our sense of will and determination, our "backbone." The negative emotion associated with the kidneys is fear. The kidneys are a strong part of our "root" system; here we experience the fear and anxiety in our lives. But now we will instill willpower and the ability to deal with our lives in a positive and creative fashion.

At this point we can sit for a few moments and allow ourselves to breathe deeply into our kidneys, located in our lower back. Each breath fills them with powerful qi so they will be able to hold us up, both in our daily lives and in all our endeavors. Our kidneys are where we store our prenatal qi or *jing*, which is very important to our physical and mental development. It is also the repository of our generative or sexual energy. Because the very pulse of life starts here, it is important that we work on creating strong kidney energy and not dissipate it through a self-abusive lifestyle.

From here the cloud moves up to the right side of the body, just below and underneath the rib cage, to the liver. Here it becomes a rich green, the green of spring, of new growth, of expansion and free-flowingness. The element is Wood, the wood of plants, grasses and trees. It is the season of spring, of new beginnings, and of outward expansion.

The liver, besides acting as a filter for the toxins in our system, regulates movement within the body. The ability for blood, qi and even emotions to move freely through the system is governed by our liver. So too it governs our ability to move freely through our emotions and our life.

As we meditate, we picture our liver being a rich green, supple and flexible, better able to help us move through the changes in our lives. We picture ourselves as the rich new growth of spring, resilient, strong and supple.

From here we can go back to the heart and cycle through again or let the energy cloud ascend back up through our head. What we have done here is pay some deep attention to the organ systems that work so well for us, moment to moment. We have thanked them for this wonderful work and we have instilled the positive qualities of cour-age, surrender, joy, free flowingness, empathy and groundedness and the will to face the changes and experiences in our life positively and creatively—certainly all valuable qualities!

Do this practice daily or whenever you feel a need to get in touch with those qualities that the organs represent. In time you will become sensitized to the health, the vitality and the inner integrity of not only your inner organs but your emotions as well.

16

Energy Is Delight
The World of Qigong

I sing the body electric!
Walt Whitman

The force that through the green fuse drives the flower drives my soul.

Dylan Thomas

To learn the Way is more important than talking about what is the Way.
Hua-Ching Ni

The term *qigong* (chee gong) is made of two characters. The first one, qi, we have learned about in the chapter on Chinese medicine. It is the basic life force of the universe; it is what animates us, what warms us, keeps our organs in their places and directs all of our movements. Mantak Chia describes qi as "the glue between our body, mind and spirit, the link between our perception of the inner and outer worlds."

The character *gong* means work or something that takes effort and time. Thus, the term qigong means working with your energy, work that will take a lot of effort and time to become fruitful. Hua-Ching Ni explains that "Chi gong is a series of movements, both internal and external, that directly activates or helps a smooth flow of chi or vital force throughout the body."

There are many different types of qigong, some quite vigorous and some sublimely simple. Effects will vary, according to the skill level of the practitioner, the consistency of the practice, his or her age and relative health. No matter what style you choose, however, all qigong deals with accessing, circulating and storing qi or vital force, within the body.

It is beyond the scope of this book to address the large and multi-layered subject of qigong thoroughly; however, more complete works on qigong are now widely available. The best way to learn it, of course, is from a personal teacher, one who will guide you as you work with energy. This is especially important for the beginning levels. There is much that can be transmitted from person to person that is all but impossible to get from a video tape or even a book.

What follows is a simple introduction to a vast and complex practice that has been in continuous practice in China for at least three thousand years and is still evolving today. A good place to start is with a form of qigong that is most familiar to Westerners: tai ji quan.

Tai Ji Quan: The Dance of Tao

Tai ji exemplifies the most subtle principle of Taoism, known as wu-wei.
Alan Watts

Tai ji is a philosophy that starts with the basic not-knowing, the basic relaxation of giving in.
Chungliang Al Huang

The purpose of doing Tai Chi is to harmonize your being.
Hua-Ching Ni

Many people in the West are familiar with the slow-moving dance-like set of movements called *tai ji quan* (tai chi chuan) or "great ulti-mate fist." Not as many people realize that it is a form of qigong. Like other forms of qigong, it works with the principles of rootedness, bal-ance, and a smooth flow of energy throughout the body. It is at once a playful dance of yin and yang and a powerful form of self-defense. The popular tai ji teacher Chungliang Al Huang says tai ji "helps you find a *moving* center. It's a movement meditation; you move your cen-ter with you. Although you are constantly in motion, you retain that quietness and stillness."

Tai ji is said to have been originally developed by a colorful old Taoist sage named Chang San Feng around 1100-1200 CE. A wonder-ful description of him from a Ming history is recorded in Yang Jwing Ming's book, *Tai Chi Chi Kung* as follows:

Chang San-Feng, from Lieu Dong Yi county. Named Chuan-Yi. Also named Jiun-Bao. San-Feng was his nickname. Because he did not keep himself neat and clean, also called Chang Lar-Tar (Sloppy Chang). He was tall and big, shaped like a turtle, and had a crane's back, large ears and round eyes. Beard long like a spear tassel. Wears only a priest's robe winter or summer. Will eat a bushel of food, or won't eat for several days or a few months. Can travel a thousand miles. Likes to have fun with people. Behaves as if nobody is around. Used to travel to Wuudang with his disciples. Built a simple cottage and lived inside.

One day after his meditation, Master Chang observed a snake coming out of its hole in the earth. Just then, a bird suddenly flew out of the sky and attacked it. After the snake and bird fought for a while, the bird flew back into the sky and the snake slithered back into its hole. Day after day he observed the same fight. History does not tell us who eventually won but it is said that by watching the continual movements of both creatures, Master Chang devised a set of movements and breathing that are now call tai ji quan. Many of the names of the movements themselves reflect their origin in the world of nature: Embrace Tiger Return to Mountain, Grasping Sparrows Tail, White Crane Spreads Its Wings, Patting the Wild Horse's Mane and so forth.

The beginnings of energy exercises can be traced to Huang Ti, the Yellow Emperor who ruled around 2700 BCE. He is said to have practiced a form of exercise called *dao in*. *Dao* means to guide and *in* means to lead. Dao in, still practiced today, is a set of prescribed movements, some spinal twists and stretches and other polarity movements, which helps to open up the qi meridians in the body and allows for smoother and stronger flow of energy there.

In the third century CE a Chinese surgeon named Hua To devised a set of movements called the Movement of Five Animals patterned after the motions of wild animals. As Daniel Reid tells us:

> In those days chee-gung was based primarily on movements learned by observing animals in nature. Arm exercises, for example, were drawn from the manner in which birds flap their wings, leg exercises imitated a tiger's gait, shoulder postures were learned from watching bears and so forth.

As various forms of movement exercises were developed over history, they were passed down through several different families, each jealously guarding their secret practices, until they eventually became common knowledge.

Each practitioner discovers for him or herself the wonders of tai ji and how it enhances our personal sense of well-being and connection to the greater source of qi. As Chungliang Al Huang likes to say, "The first tai ji master created tai ji out of the enlightenment of his own nature, out of his awareness of his body."

Fortunately it has become relatively easy to find a tai ji instructor in any town of moderate size in the West; many community colleges and community centers employ them. The challenge is finding a good one. Most instructors in the West have very little idea how to teach tai ji as a qigong practice, so many people end up learning tai ji as a relaxation method, or as a low impact aerobic exercise.

As in any physical/energetic practice, important basic principles such as rootedness, the proper alignment of the spine, how to "sink" the energy into lower dan tien and so forth are often taught incorrectly if at all. As a result the higher levels of energy movement in the body go uncommunicated or are learned incorrectly. As well, the Western urge to learn everything as fast and with as little effort as possible makes for many poor tai ji practitioners as well as instructors. As Chungliang Al Huang says:

> Unfortunately, when each master begins to teach, he may use *his* master's teaching method as he remembers it, instead of sharing with you out of his own experience *now*. Another problem is that the master may try to teach you what he can do now as a result of years of practice, instead of showing you a process that can gradually lead you to this.

To add insult to injury, we too often learn our form in a stiff and formal way. We see tai ji practitioners doing their form with a solemn frown on their faces, their movements mechanical; they are too concerned with how they look from the outside. There are even large tai ji tournaments where prizes are given for style and performance. Undoubtedly many of the winners of these awards are serious and even gifted practitioners but the emphasis on the form itself and how it looks from the outside causes many people to lose the essence of what it is they are actually practicing. As Hua-Ching Ni describes it:

> T'ai chi, in a higher and deeper level, is not a form. I described on many occasions that when you walk or do a small chore or housework, that by alternating both legs or both hands up and down, left and right, first one and then the other you are still doing t'ai chi.

Chungliang Al Huang cautions us:

> Don't make it an antiseptic, sacred, exotic, Oriental thing. Tai ji can be just as much fun as folk-dancing. You should sing inside. Tai ji is a dance in its most pure form, suspended and crystallized. It is an unlimited resource. Can you see it and feel it and hear it? Is your body moving like the sound of the ocean? Like the crackling of the fire log? The wind? The space between leaves on a tree? Or are you moving like arranged pieces of furniture, very consciously put together?

Tai ji is not just about moving your body in elegant circles. It is about being able to tap into the very flow of the universe, the dance of energy as it moves through your being and as it is expressed by you personally. Each movement is designed to move the energy in your meridians and through your body, each in a different and very precise way. In the beginning, it is very important to understand the basic principles of tai ji and to be able to build upon them so that your practice becomes a manifestation of your own personal energy system. To force yourself to move in a way that is unnatural for you is a waste of time and can even be dangerous. Find a teacher who can pass on the principles and the postures in such a way that you can make them your own, through practice, through perseverance, through a discovery of your own nature. Then you can find your own expression of tai ji, of the Tao itself.

In tai ji practice we learn how to push forward and how to yield, how to balance, first on one foot then the other, how to sink our energy deep within our bellies, our dan tien, how to maintain our composure, our inner stillness even while moving. This is why tai ji is often called "stillness within movement." It is a wonderful way to learn how to maintain our still place within the oftentimes challenging vicissitudes of life. By learning how to keep a calm and balanced center while moving backward and forward, from side to side and sometimes in a complete circle, we can learn how to maintain a sense of balance and centerdness in the rest of our lives.

We can apply the lessons we learn in tai ji practice to the rest of our lives. We can learn when it is best to push forward and when to retreat. When using tai ji for self defense we use the principle of emptiness: when someone strikes a blow at us we can sink or turn at just the right moment so that the blow is met by empty space. We can then use the momentum of that blow to pull the attacker off balance.

In tai ji practice called *tui sho* (push hands), two participants push lightly against each other in a circular motion using their hands and arms until one of them feels the other become slightly off balance. Then, a small push can throw the other completely over.

Principles that we learn in tai ji practice help us lead more harmonious and effective lives in our business relationships as well as in our personal relationships. An argument in which both sides are feeling aggressive and defensive can often escalate until one or both say or do things they later regret. By using the tai ji principles of when to be aggressive and when to retreat, or when to deflect negative energy with emptiness, the confrontation can often be defused easily.

As Chungliang Al Huang says:

Tai ji is a discipline that can help you settle into the experience of your body and your surroundings and re-establish contact with what is happening now. Then you can move out from this solid foundation of your ongoing experience.

In other words, make your tai ji practice an integral part of your life by applying the lessons you learn there to your daily experience. As Hua-Ching Ni reminds us, we can be doing tai ji even when we are not doing our official practice. Tai ji can help us learn to respond to life in a balanced and harmonious way, using the yin/yang energies in a flowing and spontaneous manner. Perhaps then we can learn to move like the animals in the forest, the birds in the sky and the fishes in the deep ocean. We can learn to move as the elements of wind, fire, water, wood and earth. We can become tai ji masters of our own lives, open to change and growth and the miracle of life unfolding all around us in a great circular and spontaneous tai ji dance.

As Hua-Ching Ni reminds us:

From movement, you find the truth that the cosmic law exists in movement. There is no stopping the procession of nature. In the movement, you experience the universe rotating and going on its way. You become a heavenly body, and you and the universe together blend to become one unified heavenly body. You join the real Heaven by always moving in a cyclical pattern of movement. All of nature is always smoothly moving along with you. You do not feel stuck in any single spot. This is high enjoyment in human spiritual life.

The Art of Qigong

As mentioned earlier, the art of qigong requires hard work and perseverance. Significant changes cannot be brought about in a single weekend workshop. It takes time to reroute the oftentimes unnatural flows of qi that have built up in our bodies. It can take years of practice to heal long lasting health problems or to build up enough vital qi so that new health problems do not occur. It can take a lifetime of practice to be able to align one's qi with the qi of the universe and be able to transcend the physical world as we know it, at the point of death or before. But all along the way there are rewards and benefits for anyone who pursues a regular practice.

The positive results can be of a physical nature, or emotional, psychological, spiritual or a combination of all four. Practicing qigong will make you healthier, more emotionally centered, more psychologically balanced, more psychic, smarter, more attractive, more creative, happier; it will strengthen your will and deepen your character—and more! This may seem unbelievable, but it is indeed true. Long-term regular practice of any kind of qigong can produce all of these results and more.

How can it work? you may ask. As with all Taoist practices, it is really quite simple. Mantak Chia affirms that "Taoist cultivation of chi energy may extend into what may at first glance appear to be impossibly subtle spiritual realms, but it always begins with down-to-earth and in-the-body practices."

Extensive research is currently being conducted in China on the effects of qigong practice. A Physiological Research Group of Shanghai First Medical College study shows that qigong practice decreases blood pressure, decreases metabolic rate and increases peristalsis. But as Daoshing Ni tells us:

> The most important discovery was that the nervous condition of the sympathetic stress reaction relaxed greatly and sympathetic impulses decreased. This indicates relaxation. This continued to a decrease of the following: arterial pressure, cellular metabolic rates, blood sugar concentration, and mental activity, and also relaxed muscular tones. After longer periods of practice, mental relaxation, ability to cope with stress, improved sleep, and a general energy increase were noted.

Other studies done in China show dramatic changes in white blood cell count. Maoshing Ni tells us:

> They found that practice actually increases production of white blood cells within 40 minutes. If you take one blood test, then practice chigong for 40 minutes and then take another blood test, there will be a jump in the number of white blood cells of around 25 to 30%. This indication of your immune system activity is dramatic and measurable.

Qigong is used regularly in hospitals all over China for the treatment of heart disease and cancer as well as for many other illnesses. A qigong hospital, the Huaxia Zhineng Qigong Clinic & Training center outside Beijing, normally houses more than four thousand people at a time. No Western medicine, no surgery, no acupuncture and no herbs are used. Instead the "students," as patients are called, practice a very simple form of qigong, treating over one hundred and eighty diseases, with an overall success rate of ninety five percent!

All qigong practice concerns accessing, circulating and storing qi as well as directing, tonifying and building a strong current of qi in the body. The various qi pathways in the body range from major meridians such as the *du mai* (flows up the back), the *ren mai* (flows down the front), the belt channel (flows around the waist) the *chong mai* (flows directly through the center of the body), the major yin channels (flow along the inside of the arms and legs), and the major yang channels (flow along the outside of the arms and legs).

Along those pathways are certain points that are used to either access or tonify the qi in that area. Several important points often used in qigong practice are the *bai hui* point at the top of the head (the crown chakra), the *tian mu* point between the eyebrows (the third eye), the *shan zhong* point (the heart center), the *wei lu* point at the bottom of the sacrum, the *hui yin* point on the perineum, the *yong quan* points at the bottoms of the feet and the *lao gong* points on the palms of the hands. When these points are energized and "opened," the qi in the pathways can run smoother and stronger.

There are also three major areas or dan tiens in the body. *Dan* means medicine or elixir and *tien* means field. The top dan tien is the third eye area, including the pineal gland. The middle dan tien is the heart area around the solar plexus. The lower dan tien is three finger widths below the navel. All of these areas are located inside of the body, rather than on the surface. As with the points, once these areas are stimulated and energized the amount of qi available to the practitioner grows manyfold.

Qigong also works with the qi field that is located both inside and outside the body. Passing the hands down the front or back of the body can affect one's internal organs because of the relationship between the outer and inner qi field. It is also how high-level martial artists can injure or even kill someone with one blow, sometimes without even touching the person! It also may explain how people described in the Bible were healed just by touching the hem of Jesus's robe. His energy field was apparently so strong that he didn't even have to be conscious of sending his healing qi out to heal someone.

Taoists see the human (*ren*) as the fulcrum between heavenly energy and earthly energy. This is why the arts of astrology and astronomy have played such an important role in Taoist science. A strong electromagnetic field produced by the planets and stars in the heavens exert a powerful influence upon us humans, and the electromagnetic power of the earth itself also exerts a strong influence upon us. We receive heavenly energy through our bai hui point at the very top of the head; we receive earthly energy through our yong chuen points at the bottoms of our feet, which are the beginning of the kidney channel, also called the Bubbling Well point. When we work with "opening" and energizing these points, we are better able to be a clear channel for heavenly and earthly energy, both for our own health and to be able to heal others. That combined with the unimpeded circulation of qi in our bodies makes us strong vital beings who can influence everyone around us.

Qigong practice, which combines deep and regular breathing, slow movements and correct visualization, can have a profound effect on our entire systems. As Daniel Reid says:

> The psychophysiological effect of performing soft, slow movements in conjunction with deep diaphragmic breathing is to switch the autonomous nervous system over from the chronically overactive sympathetic mode to the calming, restorative parasympathetic mode, in which the body's various vital functions and energies are balanced and harmonized and secretions of vital essence such as hormones and neurochemicals are stimulated.

There is an old saying that "qi follows yi," meaning that qi can be directed by the mind. Ancient Taoists knew what modern Western science is only discovering, that we can direct healing energy with our mind and effect the healing process. Experiments have been conducted in which practitioners send energy to a certain part of their bodies; that area is then measured with heat sensitive instruments. Results have shown an increase in heat radiation in the area to where the practitioner has directed qi. In the beginning stages of qigong practice we use our minds to gently guide or lead qi through the pathways and through the points we are working with. In the higher stages of practice we cease even using the mind, simply letting the qi guide itself.

An easy way to feel qi is to create a qi ball between your two palms. Hold them out in front of you at shoulder or waist height. Now imagine there is a solid ball of energy between them, about the size of a beach ball. Then gently push your hands together, squeezing the ball between them. Next, expand the ball by pulling your hands apart. Do this simple exercise a few times and you will begin to feel a subtle yet solid, rubbery presence between your palms.

Another simple yet effective exercise is to stand quietly for a few moments, then bring your arms slowly up in front of you, palms facing down, to shoulder level. Then slowly lower them to waist level. This raises your central qi to the heart center, then back down to the lower dan tien. It is an effective way to balance and center your energy. Try it at least nine times and see if you feel a difference in your sense of balance and well being.

Qigong practice not only aligns our own body/mind/spirit but also aligns us with the universal body/mind/spirit. By regulating our minds through meditation and gentle movement we can facilitate a smoother and stronger flow of energy throughout our bodies, giving us greater health and freedom of movement throughout our lives.

As with tai ji, there is a tendency to get hung up on certain qigong forms. It is essential to know that there is much more to qigong than just practicing forms. As Yang Jwang Ming says:

Always remember that Chi Kung training is not just the forms. Your feelings and comprehension are the essential roots of the entire training, this Yin side of the training has no limit, and the deeper you understand, the more you will see that there is to know.

It is challenging for most people to muster the will needed to keep up daily practice for years. In *Opening the Dragon Gate,* Master Wang Liping tells us:

Many people practicing the Way do it in the morning but then change their minds at night; they do it while sitting but then forget it when they stand up, enjoying it momentarily but tired of it in the long run, starting out diligently but winding up slacking off lazily. Their learning is not clear, their work is not earnest, their hearts are not calm, and the spirits are not true. Although they study for years, after all they don't attain; and yet they say the Great Way has turned away from humanity. In reality, it is not that the Great Way turns away from anyone; but people themselves turn their own backs on the Way.

Nowadays it is all too simple to become involved with various religious or New Age practices in a shallow and casual way. One day you're a Buddhist, the next a Sufi, the next you're channeling space beings. By contrast, qigong cultivation is a long and often slow path with inevitable bends and twists. It takes total commitment and lots of hard work to reach the highest levels of attainment. Naturally, most people are happy just to get some relief from their health issues, have their psychological or emotional issues cleared up and perhaps gain some spiritual insight into their lives. This is all fine. However, if you are truly serious about transcending the ties of the material world and "flying on the back of a dragon," then you must be resolute about your practice and try seriously to bring it into every aspect of your life.

Qigong is actually an approach to life itself. It is state of mind characterized by complete relaxation and complete acceptance, deep meditation and love, joy and beneficence, renewal and rebirth; it is open to the healing energy of the universe, and it offers healing for the whole world.

Remember the Lakota phrase *mitakuye oyasin,* "all my relatives." When we practice qigong with the intention of not only healing ourselves but of becoming a healing influence on all those around us, we begin practicing high-level qigong. One of my teachers likes to tell us that qi is love, and that we practice qigong so we can become healthier and stronger. That enables us to help others become stronger and healthier; they are then freed to help others in an unbroken and endless chain of love and qi.

It can be more challenging to find a good qigong teacher than a good tai ji teacher. There are currently many qigong books and video tapes available, some of very good quality. When interviewing a prospective teacher, it is important to ask about their own experience with qigong: find out how long they have been practicing, if they have daily practice of their own, if they know something about the meridian system, who their teacher was, and if they are properly certified to teach.

There are currently many false teachers both from China as well as from the West who are claiming great powers of healing and promising, for a fee, to perform all sorts of miraculous treatments. A word of caution: When someone seems to be charging an exorbitant rate and is making exorbitant claims, it could very well be that they are a fraud. Unfortunately most people in the West know very little, if anything, about qigong and qigong healing techniques and they can be taken advantage of very easily. Look to the appendix of this book for some organizations that can help you find a teacher or healer in your area.

Another way that qigong works is when a qigong master or healer is able to pass healing qi into a sick or injured person. Sometimes, is they are very strong, they can pass their own qi into another person but often they channel healing energy from the universe itself into their patient. In this way the patient's qi is supported and even made stronger. There are many stories in China of people being healed of all sorts of illness, including cancer, by the laying on of hands of a qigong master.

It takes a great deal of experience and training to be able to pass healing qi into another person. It can even be dangerous if the practitioner's own qi is not strong enough or of a sufficient quality to work on others. This is why most qigong masters believe that self-healing is the highest form of healing. This is not to say there aren't gifted and powerful qigong healers among us who can be very helpful with a myriad of problems. Sometimes our own qi is just too weak or stuck for us to be able to heal ourselves without outside assistance such as herbs, acupuncture or qigong therapy.

Qigong works with the forces of the universe in a clear-hearted and grounded manner in order to raise not only one's own consciousness but that of the planet itself. As Wang Liping says:

The reason Taoists value inner work is that their aim is to make dormant or latent powers and abilities become manifest. This is not mythology, but reality. Relying on such means and capacities, Taoists explore a wider, richer, more marvelous world; the work they do is a grand enterprise, one that has extremely important meaning for the present and future of humankind.

Qigong is a way to access the energy of the universe and make it our own. It is a way to help our own internal energy flow smoothly and strongly throughout our bodies. It is a way to open our spiritual eyes to be able to see beyond what our physical eyes can reach. It is an attentive, articulated attitude of openness and grace, an exchange on a deep and basic level of one's inner being and that of the great undivided, unending, undissolved Tao. And with that exchange comes balance, harmony, composure of spirit, deepening of character, relaxing of mind muscles, a feeling of safety, of being at home, of being empty and full at the same time, of being attentive to detail, clear of vision, open hearted, soft yet strong, like water, like wind, sensitive to changes in the energetic atmosphere, simple joy in beingness, compassion for the sufferings of those around you, a sense of proportion, of objectivity, openness to change, transformation and miracles.

As Hua-Ching Ni says:

> The secret to being with the Way or just learning chi movement is to enjoy yourself. The principle of Lao Tzu is *"wu wei"* which practically speaking means that if you are not too serious about high achievement, you will achieve yourself naturally just by continuing to practice.

The best way to prove the efficiacy of qigong is to simply try it yourself. Its effects will be experienced in your own being. This is much better than taking the word of an author or even teacher. Try it yourself and see what it does to your own energy. As you move deeper into your own personal practice, you will be more and more able to track the changes in your life that qigong can produce.

Chapter Sources

Walt Whitman, *Leaves of Grass*
Dylan Thomas, *Collected Poems*
Alan Watts, *The Watercourse Way*
Chungliang Al Huang, *Embrace Tiger Return to Mountain*
Hua-Ching Ni, *The Gentle Path of Spiritual Progress*
Yang Jwing Ming, *Tai Chi Chi Kung*
Daniel Reid, *The Complete Book of Chinese Health and Healing*
Hua-Ching Ni, *Mastering Chi*
Chen Kaiguo & Zheng Shunchao, *Opening the Dragon Gate*

17

Returning to the Source
Taoist Meditation

Returning to the source is a figurative term for the unutterably blissful experience of becoming aware with all one's being of perfect identity with all that is, has been or ever could be.
John Blofeld

Too few devote even one second to entering deeply the great current of life hidden within ourselves.
Mantak Chia

Let meditation assist your life, do not use it to spin a cocoon around your life.
Hua-Ching Ni

Best be still, best be empty.
In stillness and emptiness we find where to abide;
Talking and giving, we lose the place.
Lieh Tzu

Taoist meditation is often called Embracing the One or Returning to the Source. There is much about it that is mystical and may at first seem hard to understand for the beginner. But then again, as Daniel Reid so aptly puts it:

There is nothing mysterious or magical about such meditation. It is as precise, practical and effective an exercise for the mind as push-ups are for the body and breathing is for energy.

Taoist meditation is different from many other forms of Eastern meditation practices because it emphasizes energy practice over mind practice. True, we do use the mind to guide the qi, to quiet the emotions and to let go of all outside influences—those "external pernicious influences" that stir up the mud of our inner selves. But even when we are sitting still doing nothing (*ching-jing-wu-wei*) we are still running energy throughout our body or in the microcosmic orbit (up the back and down the front), or cooking up healing medicine in the cauldron of our lower dan tien. From the outside the individual appears to be sitting quietly, breathing deeply and gently, with a small half smile on his or her lips. On the inside, however, great forces are at work, reshaping and rerouting streams of energy and light, changing the entire internal being of the meditator. This internal healing energy then begins reshaping the outside. Not only do regular meditators begin to feel different, they often even look different to others. Worry lines and wrinkles begin to relax and disappear; the body, especially the spine, begins to realign itself and the meditator's posture changes. The ability to deal with life's challenges and pressures improves dramatically and so one's entire disposition changes accordingly.

The internal effects are even more dramatic. A greater sense of clarity, both emotional and psychological, begins to suffuse one's being. As qi pathways begin to unblock and the internal energy of one's body begins to travel more easily and powerfully through one's being, old illnesses and old problems begin to lighten if not disappear entirely.

As Lung Tung-pin, a Taoist immortal has described it:

As for the stages experienced through the exercise of quiescence, first there is dullness, oblivion, and random thought; then there is lightness and freshness; later it is like being inside curtains of gold mesh; finally it is like returning to life from death, a clear breeze under the bright moon coming and going, the scenery unobstructed.

Just how does one enter into this state of absolute quiescence? Lao Tzu says:

Empty yourself of everything.
Let the mind rest at peace.
The ten thousand things rise and fall while the Self watches their return.
They grow and flourish and then return to the source.
    (Chapter 16)

This is how Daniel Reid describes it:

The real point of sitting still and doing nothing is to empty the mind entirely of all conceptual thought, and let the spirit abide in emptiness, silence and stillness.

Most people in the West have a difficult time sitting still. They fidget, stretch, make noises, sway back and forth, they change posture over and over. Unfortunately, it is impossible to attain inner stillness without first attaining outer stillness. The very first prerequisite for attaining the deep levels of inner stillness and quietude needed for doing deep meditation work is that one is able to sit with spine straight for at least twenty minutes at a time.

Because this is so difficult for many beginners, the best thing to do is start with a smaller amount of time, about five minutes. After a time you can extend that period until you can sit for twenty to thirty minutes at a stretch without having to change posture or move around. Twenty or thirty minutes at a time is sufficient for most people. If your goal is to heal a serious health problem or to become an immortal then much longer periods of sitting will be necessary, but for most people a shorter period will do just fine. Taoists don't really advocate long uninterrupted hours of sitting for most people. It is said to cause the inner energy to stagnate in the organs and can actually do more harm than good. I was once told by a Taoist master that too much sitting will make your teeth fall out!

It is very important to keep the spine erect and straight, not as if at attention but as if there were a string pulling you up from the top of your head, from the bai hui point at the center of the crown while pulling in your chin slightly. This way the energy coming up the du mai channel, which runs up the back of the spine, can flow evenly and smoothly.

As to the actual sitting practice—it is important that one does not slump or fidget but it is equally important that one does not hold one's self too stiffly. As Hua-Ching Ni says:

If your attitude towards meditation is too tight and you sit solemnly and stiffly, you will nourish and increase this overly serious and unpleasant aspect of your practice and this will become the sour fruit you bear. If, on the other hand, you sit with genuine joy, the world sings to you; the pores and cells of the breeze dance for you.

After mastering sitting still and keeping the spine erect, the next step is breathing correctly. Breathing is something most people feel they can do very well already, but actually, most people don't do a very good job of breathing at all. They breathe mostly from the upper part of the chest, and so don't utilize their actual lung power to the fullest. According to Dennis Lewis in his work, *The Tao of Natural Breath-*

ing, though our lungs have a total air capacity of about 5,000 milliliters, the average breath is only about 500 milliliters.

There is a very large muscle right above our abdominal cavity called the diaphragm. As Dennis Lewis describes it:

> Shaped like a large dome, the diaphragm functions as both the floor of the chest cavity and the ceiling of the abdominal cavity. It is penetrated by—and can affect—several important structures, including the esophagus, which carries food to the stomach; the aorta, which carries blood from the heart to the arteries of all the limbs and organs except the lungs; the vena cava, the central vein that carries various nerves including the vagus nerve, which descends from the medulla oblongata and branches to the various internal organs.

When we breathe correctly, from the belly, filling our lungs from the bottom up, we also work that diaphragm muscle, massaging our digestive organs and promoting the flow of blood and lymph to that region. Also, by breathing slowly and deeply we are better able to arrive at a sense of peacefulness and centeredness. Thus, by simply breathing correctly one can obtain peacefulness, a sense of groundedness and centerdness and promote better digestion and respiration.

Probably the most basic form of breathing in Taoist meditation or other qigong practices is what is called Natural Breathing or Prenatal Breathing. The idea is to breathe into the belly or the lower dan tien as if we are babies breathing in our mother's womb, not through our lungs but through our umbilical cord. In other words, when we breathe in our abdomen expands; when we exhale our abdomen contracts. Of course, all breathing is done through the nose, which is specifically designed for warming and filtering the air before it gets to our lungs.

This is a very calming type of breathing. If you practice breathing in this way for even fifteen minutes a day, you will eventually begin breathing this way all of the time, even when you are sleeping, and the benefits will be enormous.

We are all familiar with the "flight or fight" feeling we get when we are alarmed or in shock. What happens to our breath? It pretty much stops or becomes very shallow. If we pause for a moment to take a few really slow and deep breaths when we find ourselves in a stressful situation, it can often clear our mind and quiet our nervous system, helping us to better handle the situation.

There are numerous other, more esoteric breathing practices used in Taoist inner alchemical practices. Extensive literature in the Taoist Canon describes various breathing practices, some extremely difficult and requiring the guidance of a teacher. But for basic Taoist meditation practices such as sitting or even tai ji, the Natural Breath is sufficient. Practice it daily and you will be amazed at the sublime effects this simple practice can produce.

How many of you have seen statues of the Buddha, the Awakened One, sitting in meditation? Notice the little half smile on his face? He's not sitting there like a lump of wood, solemn and stiff. We need to sit with that same spirit of joy and openness. One of the things I remember most about my first tai ji teacher, David Cheng, was the warm smile he held all through his practice. In Taoism, we believe that it's quite alright to enjoy our practices, that spiritual work can be fun! So relax those facial muscles, and let a small smile play about your lips as you sit. Remember, it takes a lot more muscles to frown than it does to smile.

Energy in the body travels along very specific pathways. Two of the main pathways are the du mai and the ren mai. The du mai runs up the back of the body and the ren mai runs down the front of the body. The place where they meet is in the upper and lower palate in the mouth. In meditation, as in all qigong practices, we want to connect those two pathways by placing the tongue lightly upon the upper palate. This connects up the two pathways much like a completed electrical circuit. This way the qi or internal energy can circulate in an efficient manner.

Placing the tongue on the palate also produces greater amounts of saliva. Taoists think saliva is a precious substance, and it is often called such fanciful names as Golden Dew. Dennis Lewis tells us that:

> Science has shown that saliva contains a wide variety of proteins, including hormones and other substances, that have digestive, antibacterial, mineral-building, and other health functions.

It is also thought that correct breathing fills our saliva with qi, which we can then swallow down into our internal organs. Whenever we have accumulated a good amount of saliva we should swallow it forcefully, imagining that it is traveling all the way into our lower dan tien, our field of elixir. There are certain practices where one rolls the tongue around the inside of the mouth in order to accumulate a good amount of saliva and then separates the mouthful of saliva into three parts and swallows them each separately, sometimes down different sides of the abdomen and then the center. Suffice it to say that saliva should not be viewed as a nasty waste product but a vital, healthful substance that we can use for our own benefit.

Once you have learned about sitting still, straight and smiling, you can begin your meditation. Many people have the mistaken notion that meditation is solely for the purpose of quieting the mind. They suppose that if they sit long enough, trying very hard not to think, eventually they will begin to turn off their brain and cease thinking altogether, thereby entering into enlightenment. Taoists have a different view. The trick is to get the mind out of the way so that the qi can move in its own fashion.

Taoist meditation masters created moving meditation forms such as tai ji in order to find a way for people to move in a slow and flowing meditative state and allow the qi in their bodies to move on its own. Tai ji is often called "stillness within movement." In still sitting there is also a "movement within stillness." As Taoist master Gu Jiaoyi put it:

> After you enter into quiet stillness sitting cross-legged, once random thoughts are eliminated, when stillness reaches its extreme, it produces movement.

This inner movement is the healing, vitalizing qi moving deep within the three dan tiens, opening energy pathways as well as spiritual centers. It is also how we find our deep connection with the eternal. The more we dwell within that state the easier it is to have it carry over into the rest of our lives.

All Taoist practices are about refining our energy, our qi, our mind. This refinement process has many levels—psychological, emotional and spiritual. It is also concerned with the internal alchemical process of refining our jing or fundamental energy, into qi and then refining that into pure spiritual energy or shen and then transforming that back into the the Tao. It is a slow process, taking many years of serious practice to fully accomplish. But there are many helpful results that occur along the way, making the practice itself a rewarding and educational process.

There are many different kinds of meditation. Some are for stilling the mind and slowing down the rat race course of random thinking the Buddhists call the monkey mind. Other kinds are for building vital energy and then circulating that within the body. Others are for reaching a state of oneness with the infinite, or the great unending Tao itself. Other times we may enter a state of quiet meditation to work on some problem in our life or when we have an important decision to make.

Many people find it very difficult to enter a deep state of meditation because their monkey mind is so full of thoughts which lead to other thoughts which lead to others and so on and on. It can be helpful to count your breaths from one to ten, concentrating fully on each count. Then, once you reach ten, go back and start over again. In the beginning it is often difficult to count much past ten without the monkey mind starting up again.

We can utilize the power of quietude and stillness to be better able to hear the inspiration and guidance of our higher self, or our guardian or helping spirits. Taoists, like Native Americans and many other primal peoples, believe that we are surrounded by helpful spirit guides at all times, though they are very hard to hear above the usual symphony of noise that plays in our heads most of the time. We need to become quiet inside in order to hear the "still small voice within" and benefit from the guidance we receive.

Hua-Ching Ni says:

The truth never fears being tested. When you sit to meditate, you need to sit with something in your mind that will strengthen the conception of your own spiritual being. You can't sit empty-minded or you will turn to stone. You want to bear happy, living fruit. Who needs a sour apple?

Or as qigong teacher Hui Xian Chen says:

To me, to do meditation is not just to sit there and be blank. I think a lot. It is important to think, because the mind is for thinking. Either you think of money, you think of doing things, you think of work, think of shopping, or marrying and so on. Why not think of the big things which are more important to you? That is, where does life come from, where does it go? What should you do this lifetime, why are we all here? This is more important.

Much of what we know today as the meridian system, which is used in Chinese medicine and qigong practice, was mapped by those "inner astronauts" the ancient Taoists, who while sitting in deep meditation, were able to track how and where energy moved in their bodies. When I was a kid I had a model called The Visible Man; it was a human body with clear skin which enabled me to see all the inner organs. The ancient Taoists had their own form of Visible Man because they were able to open, with their inner vision, windows into their own bodies and see how they worked, all without the aid of dissection!

As Daniel Reid says:

While Western science had to wait until the development of equipment sufficiently sensitive to observe, measure and record light waves, electric pulses and atomic particles, Taoists simply "sat still and did nothing" long enough to awaken their own inner reflections of the universe.

Lao Tzu says that:

Without going outside, you may know the whole world.
Without looking through the window, you may see the ways of heaven.
(Chapter 47)

Using our inner vision we are better able to see our true path in life, are better able to travel through the wilds of our emotional landscape, and traverse the deep rivers and ravines of our inner being and arrive back home, back to our eternal source, back to Tao.

A typical meditation session would go like this: First, sit on a cushion high enough and firm enough to give support to your lower back, or sit on the front part of a chair with your feet planted firmly on the floor. It is extremely important to keep your spine erect yet not stiff. Never slump on your cushion or chair. Next, bounce around for a moment, letting the unprocessed energy of the day settle down in your body. Then exhale deeply and suddenly, emptying your lungs fully. Take three deep breaths, then either close your eyes or keep them in a half closed position and unfocused.

Many people find that closing their eyes helps them shut out extraneous distraction from the outside world. The danger is that one may be tempted to "zone out" or even fall asleep. Taoist meditation is not about going into a trance or falling asleep. Instead it is a form of dynamic interaction between our outer and inner selves. As Deng Ming Dao says:

> Meditation is not possible for the unimaginative, the stupid, or the dogmatic. Meditation requires a plunging into the creative, a suspension of the everyday logical mind that stands in the way of our efforts. It is only when we go behind this petty, rationalistic mind that extraordinary experiences become possible.

Watch a cat sometime. Notice how she sits or lies with eyes half closed or closed, completely relaxed, seemingly deeply asleep. But let a squirrel or bird come anywhere in her vicinity and she's up like a shot. She has been engaged in a deeply relaxed meditative state yet is able to awaken with no effort and can move with great speed and agility at a moment's notice.

Taoists are great believers in learning from animals. Many famous qigong forms such as Soaring Crane, Wild Goose and Five Animal Frolics were created after watching how various animals moved in their native habitat. Not that we expect you to start chasing squirrels! But observing how animals move and conduct themselves, especially in the wild, has always been of great use to Taoist practitioners.

There is no need to be rigid or dogmatic about posture. Either sitting cross-legged on a cushion or even in a half lotus, if you can manage it, is sufficient. The main idea is to feel balanced and stable. You don't want to be so relaxed that you topple over to one side or the other; neither do you want to sit too stiffly and end up with a sore back. Deep relaxation is imperative. As Deng Ming Dao says:

> Relaxation is an imperative prelude to all breathing exercises and to medi-
> tation. You should relax your body completely, part by part if necessary. You
> must also relax your mind by putting aside the worries of the day and by
> looking forward to your practice with an open attitude free of anxiety.

Correct relaxation is not collapse. It is an energetic, dynamic type
of relaxation in which your muscles, tendons, organs, and nervous system get a chance to refresh and re-energize themselves. Many people,
if they allow themselves to totally relax, find themselves falling asleep
or nodding out. It is very important to reach a state of dynamic relaxation for meditation or any other type of qigong practice to be truly
effective. Again, Deng Ming Dao:

> Relaxation does not mean loss of control. Relaxing your body doesn't mean
> letting it go limp. It means dispelling all tension, and allowing the inherent
> energy of your body to flow freely. In this sense, relaxation releases energy.

Remember the cat. Relax your shoulders, and begin to breath deeply
and slowly, from the belly. Remember to place the tip of your tongue
on your upper palate, relax your face into a small smile and let yourself be breathed.

Remember, "qi follows yi" or qi follows the mind. It is an ancient
and well-known fact that we can lead energy in the body with our
minds. There is even a relatively new branch of Western medicine called
psychoneuroimmunology, which means basically the same thing. For
example, patients with tumors are taught to send little white knights
or pac man type mouths to defeat or eat up the rampaging cancer cells
in their body, often to great effect.

So the idea is to place the mind or our attention onto our lower
dan tien and allow ourselves to feel our breath, our qi, flowing into our
body and then back out again in a slow, rhythmic way. Feel yourself
fill up with good, clean, healing qi and then feel yourself exhale all the
old, unclean, used up qi. Just relax and let it happen by itself, no effort,
no tension, no desire, no agenda, no goal. Just let yourself be carried
on the wings of energy and of the Tao itself. Let yourself sink deeply
into the still, quiet depths of your own being.

When your time is up or you feel that your sense of inner quietude
is beginning to dissolve, bring your palms in front of you and rub them
together briskly thirty-six times; place them over your eyes, inhaling
the warmth of your palms deep into your eyes and brain; then rub
them gently or briskly up and down over your face three times. When
you are finished sit for a moment or so with your palms placed over

your lower dan tien, below your navel. Let the warmth of your palms enter your dan tien, storing up the good warm, healing qi there.

Be careful how you re-enter the world after deep meditation. Try not to have to jump right into your workaday world immediately. Take at least five minutes to gather your energy. If you can, sit down and drink a cup of tea or do some gentle stretching or go in and wash some dishes, slowly and carefully. Avoid talking with other people too soon. You will be in a heightened and extremely sensitive state at this time; if you plunge too quickly into your everyday life or if you encounter a tense situation or energy exchange with someone else, you will feel it very deeply and be easily knocked off balance. So take it easy with yourself, like the cat who stretches fully (when she is not chasing the squirrel), yawns deeply a few times and then slowly enters the outer world on her own terms.

Chapter Sources

John Blofeld, *Gateway to Wisdom*
Hua-Ching Ni, *Spring Thunder*
A.C. Graham, *The Book of Lieh-tzu*
Daniel Reid, *The Tao of Health, Sex, & Longevity*
Thomas Cleary, *The Taoist I Ching*
Gia Fu-Feng & Jane English, *Tao Te Ching*
Hua-Ching Ni, *The Gentle Path of Spiritual Progress*
Dennis Lewis, *The Tao of Natural Breathing*
Deng Ming Dao, *Scholar Warrior*

18

Under Golden Pond

The Tao may be likened to a great pool of still water, deep, dark and eternally calm. It is in this great pool that each one of us is born, lives out our lives, and then dies. We never leave it.

Picture yourself as a little frog sitting quietly on a lily pad which floats gently on the surface of this pond. It is a bright, hot day and the sounds of the world are loud and cacophonous. Planes fly overhead, cars whoosh by, the sound of voices of children in play and adults in argument waft over you from the other side of the pond.

Finally, after listening to the barrage of noise for long enough, you gently plop yourself over the edge of the lily pad and allow yourself to sink into the depths of the pond.

Down and down you go, effortlessly sinking ever deeper into the warm, dark depth of the pond. Down you go through the layers, past swiftly darting fish and slowly lumbering turtles, past the gracefully waving arms of underwater plants you go, like a little weighted doll, until at last you sink to the bottom.

At first it is very muddy, as your presence churns up the silt and sediment that lies on the bottom of the pond. You can't really see anything but can only sit, listening to the quiet thump of your heart. Sounds are indistinct also. The rush of the world is far above you now and doesn't affect you anymore. You feel the smooth current of the water dancing all around you.

But as the silt and mud sink back down to the bottom and the water gradually clears you can, perhaps for the first time, see clearly everything surrounding you. The water is warm and soothing. You sit very still, enveloped in this great soothing, motherly world of water. You breathe slowly and deeply, drawing the healing water into your belly. Your breath slows down until you yourself are breathed, the rhythm of breath itself taking over. Your heartbeat slows down also, matching your breath, matching the rhythm of nature, of the Tao.

All worldly cares slip away as you are enfolded into a vast and limitless world where you as an individual are no longer important. The small self you have clung to all your life recedes into a much grander sense of Self, of connection to something larger and more eternal. The little pond you sit in expands outward to become a great sea of qi, of life. You sit here, suspended effortlessly, eternally present in an eternal moment of clarity and wisdom.

After a time you release a little bubble of qi into the water and begin your ascent back into the world. You float up slowly through the layers of the water all the way back to the surface where you plop yourself onto your lily pad, renewed, refreshed, released and begin your life again.

Who can sit quietly while the mud settles?
Who can remain still until the moment of action?
                Lao Tzu (Chapter 15)

19

Deepening Your Practice

To learn the Way is more important than talking about what is the Way.
Hua-Ching Ni

The Abbot of Loukuantai, a venerable and delightful old man, said to me: "The world thinks that it is going forward and that we Taoists are going backward, but really it is just the opposite; we are going forward and they are going backward."
Joseph Needham

Standing firmly upon the earth, feet flat on the ground, pulling up the good yin energy of the earth through my yong chuen points, knees slightly bent, spine straight, bai hui pointing up to pull in good yang energy from heaven, "thinking of nothing" and smiling slightly, I begin my morning practice.

Facing south, I inhale slowly into my dan tien, building up qi there until I begin to circulate it up my du mai, through da zui and down to my palms. From there I move it out to the south, then to the west and the east. I reach up to exchange qi with heaven, then bend down to exchange qi with the earth, creating a vortex of energy that I will move within for the rest of my practice.

Gathering, circulating and spreading qi throughout my body, I become stronger, healthier, more at peace with myself and my surroundings. The lessons the qi teaches me are the lessons of my life. I am more whole, more balanced and more creative since I have begun practicing qigong. Now it is time to share that energy with others.

In the beginning of each qigong class I teach, I explain the basic concepts of qi, qi circulation and why we do qigong. "Qigong is a state of mind," I tell my students. "It is a state of being, a state of grace." We do not practice qigong for only thirty minutes a day; we practice it in everything we do—in our personal relationships, our business relationships, our family, our communities and in our quest for unity with the divine, the Tao.

We begin with meditation, so that we can start from a place of peace and harmony. Then we begin to move. At first it seems too complicated—so many moves, so difficult! The students are sure they will never remember this. But little by little, as we work through the day, their bodies become used to the movements and they become a little more sure of themselves.

By the second day the first two sections seem easy now, or at least possible. The students begin to move more confidently, and they are more balanced and poised. At this point, because they are trying so hard to remember the sequence of movements, they are not yet aware of qi moving through their bodies. But I know with perseverance they will begin to tap into and enjoy the feeling of moving in that qi space, the place of harmony and connection to the life force surrounding us.

Teaching helps me learn my lessons more thoroughly. It has been said that one teaches what one most needs to learn. I know that is true for me. The dedication, the discipline, the perseverance to sustain a regular practicee, the openness to learning and experiencing deeper and deeper levels of the practice, the ability to share and inspire others—all of this is what I need to learn as deeply and thoroughly as I can.

The *Tao Te Ching* describes how the Universe was created. In the beginning, it says, there was Tao, undifferentiated consciousness. Then *Tao sheng yi*, the Tao gives birth to the one, the oneness. When we first start doing our form, we stand and center ourselves. We put our roots deep into the earth. We breathe into our lower dan tien. We relax our whole body part by part. We stay that way for a few minutes. We ground ourselves. We balance ourselves. That's the one.

Then, *yi sheng erh*. The one gives birth to the two, yin and yang, the polarity of the universe. Now we begin to exchange energy. We pull clean, fresh, healing energy into ourselves; we push the "dirty" used energy out. First there is oneness, no movement. Then there is movement. This is how the Universe comes into being.

Next, *erh sheng san*, the two gives birth to the three—the jing, the qi, and the shen or earth, human, heaven.

Then the last part says *san sheng ru ee*, which means the three gives birth to the ten thousand things, all of material reality. It is in the transformative power of the polarity of yin and yang along with the interaction of the earthly energy, the human energy and the heavenly energy that the world of cause and effect, what we experience as the material plane, comes into being. So by entering the oneness then engaging the yin and yang energy exchange we create a whole world—the world of qigong, the world of our new selves.

Each movement arises from a place of complete stillness and peace. Like small ripples spreading slowly across a still pond, our movements rise up and then return to that same place of complete stillness and peace. Remember, qigong and tai ji practice are called "stillness within movement." Within our movement our center is completely still and at peace.

There is another level yet, however. Within our movement is that still place. Within that still place is yet another place of movement. That is where we access the true qi. Just as within our still meditation, when our outer form is still, there is a place of movement—our qi is moving through the pathways of our bodies, replenishing and regenerating us. Then within that place of movement, there is yet another level of stillness. This is where the medicine, the elixir is made.

This is a deep teaching. Many people, believing they know all about stillness in movement and movement in stillness, think they understand internal alchemy. But to attain the alchemical state where jing, or prenatal qi, can be transformed into qi, the qi transformed into pure spirit or shen, and then that transformed back into the original primordial Tao, we must reach deeper levels of practice. This takes time and effort, the "gong" of qigong. When we reach a place of utter stillness within the movement within the stillness in our meditation, then we can begin that process of refinement and transformation.

In *The Book of Balance and Harmony*, a thirteenth century collection of Taoist writings translated by Thomas Cleary, it says:

> Thus the cycle of work goes from movement to stillness to movement to stillness. With long perseverance in practice, there takes place a gradual solidification, a gradual crystallization, which is the stabilization of real consciousness. This is described as nonsubstance producing substance, and it is represented as a spiritual embryo. This is called completion of the elixir.

Much of Taoist internal alchemy work is couched in poetic and often obtuse metaphors such as "mercury within cinnabar," "overcoming the dragon and subduing the tiger," and "producing the golden embryo" or "the red baby." This last refers to a state in which one's internal energy is so refined that a new materialization of pure spiritual energy is created, a spiritual baby that floats above one's head. It can also be thought of as projection of one's internal spiritual essence. It is said that if one is able to produce such a spiritual infant that, upon one's death, it will continue to live for eternity.

Taoists talk about using the cauldron of the lower dan tien to cook up the medicine, the elixir of eternal life. Numerous descriptions, couched in symbolic and archaic language, tell how this process works. Much of Taoist internal alchemy uses this highly symbolic and difficult to understand terminology. This was in part an attempt to hide the true teachings from the uninitiated, and in part a way to use words to describe the indescribable. Even today scholars disagree on just what was meant in any one passage of internal alchemical texts.

It is important to remember that in spite of the highly esoteric and symbolic language, the process itself is very simple. By entering a state of complete stillness, the internal movement is able to reach the deepest levels of our being to produce the spiritual awakening, the elixir of immortality.

As *The Book of Balance and Harmony* says:

Gathering medicine means gathering the true sense of the essence of consciousness within oneself. This is done by first using the mind to still the impulses of arbitrary feelings; when stillness is perfected, there is a movement of unconditioned energy.

In the beginning stages of internal alchemy we talk about certain centers such as the three dan tiens, or specific points such as tian mu or the third eye point. In reality, there is no specific spiritual center or point within the body. The center is a moving center. The so-called "mysterious pass" is not located in any one specific place in the body. *The Book of Balance and Harmony* quotes an alchemical text that says:

The opening of the mysterious pass is not to the right or the left, not in front or back, not above or below, not on the inside or outside, not on either side, not in the middle. It is the point where the physical elements and five forces do not adhere.

The true spiritual center is not the belly, heart or third eye. It is where thought is born, where spirit is joined with energy, where energy is transformed into spirit, where spirit is transformed into oneness and before the oneness, back to the Tao itself. In higher level practice we cease to concentrate on any one spot or point or center. This is when our thoughts cease to be born, when our energy is gathered and refined to a pure pearl of spiritual reality, when we can then expand that pearl into our entire being, when we are no longer identified with being a "spiritual seeker" or student of anything at all, when we let go of all pre-conceived notions of spiritual reality. When we can become as a newborn babe—innocent, pure and innately curious and open to all experience—we can begin to reach the place the Taoists call Returning to the Source.

The Book of Balance and Harmony likens us to a puppet, whose every act is controlled by our strings which are, in turn controlled by the puppet master. The puppet is the body, the strings are the "mysterious pass" or the spiritual center and the puppet master is the innermost self. It tells us that:

The movements of the body are not done by the body; it is the mysterious pass that makes it move. But though it is the action of the mysterious pass, still it is the innermost self that activates the mysterious pass. If you can recognize this activating mechanism, without a doubt you can become a wizard.

This is magic of the highest order. Once you can understand just who it is that is pulling the strings, you can free yourself from them. Like Pinocchio, you can leave off being a puppet, a victim, an unconscious being sleepwalking through life and become what Chuang Tzu calls a Real Man or Woman, a sage, a wizard, an enlightened being.

This is not a path for the faint hearted or the weekend spiritual seeker. It is for someone who wishes to use their cultivation for every aspect of their life—from health to sexuality, from how they make their living to how they treat their fellow workers, from how they approach politics to how they approach their family. It takes dedication and willingness to take chances.

Wang Liping says:

If you want to learn the Way, just be ready to work hard. Otherwise, how can you rise above the ordinary human condition? The first requirement for learning the Way is hard work; then you need to learn to be a member of society, which means doing good and refraining from evil, building up character. When you have developed virtue and built up character, eventually you enter naturally into the Way.

Also, when we do a moving form, when we can really feel and experience the sense of the deep elemental movement within the stillness within our outer movements, we can begin to feel and experience what all the ancient achieved ones described as "riding on the back of a dragon."

The Book of Balance and Harmony says:

For harmonious attunement, movement is valuable; for careful concentration, stillness is valuable. Movement is patterned on heaven, stillness is patterned on earth; when body and mind are both calm, heaven and earth join.

And:

When the work reaches this point, body and mind merge, movement and stillness complement each other, and the mechanism of opening and closing of heaven and earth is entirely within oneself. Eventually the mind returns to open quiescence and the body enters nondoing; movement and stillness are both forgotten, vitality stabilizes, and energy transmutes.

Taoist practice can take you as far as you possibly wish to go. If you wish better health, a more balanced lifestyle and so forth, you can achieve that. If you want to become a healer and affect other people's energy and organ systems, you can do that. If you want to become a teacher of Taoist arts, you can do that. If you want to become an immortal and leave the restrictions of the material world behind, you can do that. All it takes is the right guidance, and the perseverance on your part to do the practices in a dedicated and serious way.

Lao Tzu says:

Knowing others is wisdom;
Knowing the self is enlightenment.
Mastering others requires force;
Mastering the self needs strength.
          (Chapter 33)

Taoists believe in reaching the infinite or enlightenment *through the body*. This means that we can use the intrinsic energies of our own bodies to refine ourselves to become wiser, lighter, and more compassionate beings. In ancient times a number of emperors in China died by ingesting highly poisonous substances while searching for the elixir of immortality. What they didn't understand is that the elixir of immortality is within us. When we work to refine our gross energy into a finer and finer level of attainment we begin to lose our strong attachment to the material world. It no longer has such a strong hold on us. We are able to look at life with an objectivity previously unavailable to us. We are no longer subject to "the slings and arrows of outrageous fortune" but instead create our own destiny, moment by moment.

Of course to work in the deeper realms of Taoist practice it is essential to have a teacher. Many of the practices are extremely difficult and sometimes dangerous to the uninitiated. The important thing is to go slowly. The Taoist is someone who never seems to be in a hurry about anything, yet gets everything done.

Lao Tzu describes him or her thusly:

In the universe the difficult things are done as if they are easy.
In the universe great acts are made up of small deeds.
The sage does not attempt anything very big,

And thus achieves greatness.
                (Chapter 63)

In the same chapter he also says:

Because the sage always confronts difficulties,
He never experiences them.

Lao Tzu teaches us to deal with problems while they are still small, when it is easy. If we wait too long they become big problems and difficult to deal with. We must remain flexible like the bamboo, soft like the water and open-minded as the wind in order to move through life and its challenges in a graceful and harmonious way.
      Again Lao Tzu cautions us:

A man is born gentle and weak.
At his death he is hard and stiff.
Green plants are tender and filled with sap.
At their death they are withered and dry.

Therefore the stiff and unbending is the disciple of death.
The gentle and yielding is the disciple of life.
                (Chapter 76)

      To be a Taoist is to remain "gentle and weak, tender and yield-ing." In this way we can overcome suffering and the obstacles life thrusts at us. We can connect with our own "true nature," our own natural, joyous, childlike selves. To choose Taoism is to say a great re-sounding "yes" to life, to change, to nature and ultimately, to our own sweet enduring selves, our own unique and special expression of the Tao.
      Or, as John Blofeld puts it:

A mind fed on words such as heaven, earth, dew, essence, cinnabar, moon-light, stillness, jade, pearl, cedar, and winter-plum is likely to have a serenity not found in minds ringing with the vocabulary of the present age—computer, tractor, jumbo jet, speed ball, pop, dollar, liquidation, napalm, overkill! Who would thrill at the prospect of rocketing to the moon in a billion-dollar space-craft if he knew how to summon a shimmering gold and scarlet dragon at any time day or night and soar among the clouds? And how full of wisdom is a philosophy that draws man away from the rat-race, from the tooth-and-claw struggle for status, wealth, power or fame, to live frugally and contentedly in harmony with nature, reaching effortlessly for the tranquillity that flowers in a heart nurtured in stillness!

Besides doing our practices and having the right attitude about change and challenge, it is important to nurture our natural virtue. Wang Liping says:

> ...the highest virtue is spontaneous, formless, invisible, imperceptible; it is internal, stored within, not revealed obviously. It is not intentional but natural. . . . To go through ordinary life with the virtue of a sage, mixing in with the mundane world, is an even higher level of life, referred to as "transcending sagehood to enter the ordinary."

Our natural virtue is what will support us throughout our cultivation. Virtue is more than just doing good deeds. It is an attitude of openness of heart and mind. It is the willingness to share what we have learned and experienced with others, in a humble and warm hearted way.

Lao Tzu describes it as follows:

> Cultivate Virtue in your self,
> And Virtue will be real.
> Cultivate it in the family,
> And Virtue will abound.
> Cultivate it in the village,
> And Virtue will grow.
> Cultivate it in the nation,
> And Virtue will be abundant.
> Cultivate it in the universe,
> And Virtue will be everywhere.
>   (Chapter 54)

Wang Liping says:

> ...cultivating essential nature is more than cultivating life. To do good deeds without expecting reward is for building up virtue; when virtue is high, attainment also rises.

Gone are the days when spiritual seekers need to retreat to the mountains in order to cultivate themselves. Now is the time for cultivation within society, thereby uplifting society as well. We all need to learn our lessons and practice our deep spiritual cultivation within the world as it is. Master Lu Dong-bin, an ancient Taoist master said:

> Without spending a penny or wasting an ounce of effort, one achieves it by merely sitting. Without another soul being aware, our power rivals that of nature itself. Thus it is that with our own selves we can save the whole world.

Remember, your cultivation is not merely yours alone. It is for everyone around you. You don't have to be healing people or teaching workshops or writing books to have an effect on the world. By being true to your cultivation in all aspects of your life you can "save the whole world."

Many teachers, both in China and in the West, concentrate on teaching forms. Many students then get the mistaken notion that qigong is all about forms. They begin to collect forms and teachers, sometimes debating with other students whose form or teacher is better.

What they don't understand is that if they wish to attain the deepest levels of spiritual cultivation, at some point they will have to leave the forms behind. We learn forms in order to access the qi. Once we access the qi we can leave the world of forms behind. Most modern qigong forms in China have a section built into them which allows for spontaneous movement. In spontaneous qigong it is the qi which directs the movement. No longer is the mind or intent directing the qi. It is the qi itself moving in its own way.

True cultivation is concerned not with forms or meditation techniques but with going beyond all techniques. Liu Cao, a disciple of Lu Dongbin wrote:

Don't think holding your breath is a true exercise; even counting breaths and contemplating designs are not. Even if you have cast off external concerns, if you still have inner mental entanglements, what is the difference in either case? Just observe the baby in the womb—does it know how to make subconscious calculations? Unify your energy and make it flexible, and the spirit will be permanently stabilized. The true breath going and coming is naturally unhurried, an extended continuum traveling around, returning to original life. Then even though you do not draw on it, the spiritual spring spontaneously flows at all times.

Real cultivation is only possible in true stillness. In order to be able to refine our energy into more and more subtle levels we must be able to still the mind, soften the heart and enter into the deep levels of stillness where we can begin to let the medicine be made. Running from one teacher to another, one spiritual path to another, one practice to another will not accomplish this. We must find a way to come to a complete stop and let the world rush by as we sink ever deeper into the deepest realms of spiritual cultivation. We need to let go of all fear, all attachment, all hope of progress, all personal theories of spiritual reality and let qi guide us into ever more refined levels of being. Eventually, after long years of practice, our energy will become transformed, we will become transformed, and in this way the world will become transformed.

Eventually what happens is that you are able to apply the experiences and knowledge that you have gained through your practice to the rest of your life. Then, like Hua-Ching Ni says, you can be doing your tai ji while doing housework. You can be doing qigong while driving. Even the act of writing this book has been a practice of qigong for me—it has been a process of gathering, storing, refining and transforming information and ideas. You readers will then be able to absorb the ideas, the information and the qi of the various teachers quoted and what small amount of wisdom I have been able to attain myself.

In the higher or deeper levels of practice, you don't need to be thinking about specific centers or points or pathways. The qi itself becomes the teacher. It will lead you to where you need to be in order to learn and to grow and to become a more balanced and wiser being.

"The deep truth cannot be learned from books alone," says Hua-Ching Ni, "but as a direct subtle revelation in your own sagely mind." Once we are on our Way we will find teachers everywhere. We will learn lessons, some easy, some difficult, in everything that we do. We will be able to seamlessly apply to the rest of our lives whatever we learn in our meditation, our tai ji practice, our qigong practice, and our reading.

Chapter Sources

Hua-Ching Ni, *Mastering Chi*
Joseph Needham, *Science and Civilization in China*
Gia-Fu Feng and Jane English, *Tao Te Ching*
Chen Kaiguo and Zheng Schunchao, *Opening the Dragon Gate*
John Blofeld, *Taoism, the Road to Immortality*
Douglas Wile, *The Chinese Sexual Yoga Classics*
Thomas Cleary, *The Book of Balance and Harmony*
Hua-Ching Ni, *Spring Thunder*

20

On Our Way

A journey of a thousand miles starts under one's feet.
Tao Te Ching

What, in the end, are we left with? Can the seeds of Taoism be sown successfully in the West? Many people, students and teachers alike, believe so. They are dedicating themselves to the task of integrating Taoist philosophy and practice into Western culture. For, as we have seen, Taoism is the least "ism"-like path of all. In its connection to nature, to exploring the inner dimensions of experience, its reliance on "soft" technology, and its adherence to direct experience and avoidance of dogma, Taoism has the potential to have a large and creative influence on modern culture.

In the last four years of publishing *The Empty Vessel* magazine, I have met with many students of the Way and even a few masters. Common to all of them is an openness of vision, a willingness to experiment, a devotion to regular practice, and an approach to life based on working with the forces of change rather than against them.

I can foresee a future in which qigong, both as a personal practice and as a form of healing, will be an accepted part of our society. I see a time when Taoist energy meditation techniques are taught in grammar schools. Already in China, studies have been conducted in which young children are taught simple qigong exercises and then their grades are tracked. It's no surprise to me that the regular exercises have caused their grades to improve.

Lao Tzu said that a journey of a thousand miles begins with the first step. The first time you sit down to meditate, the first tai ji or qigong class you attend, the first time you sit down with Chuang Tzu, the first time you take a walk in the forest and feel the qi of the trees emanating toward you, the first time you allow yourself to expand your sense of self into the greater Self, the first time you attempt to use sex for spiritual cultivation—any of these can be the first step on a very long and adventurous journey.

Except for brief periods in China, Taoists have always lived outside the general society. Needham describes them as "the rebel, the recluse, the rogue and the returnist." They were individualists who wanted no part of the rigid Confucian society of their time and were not interested in being proper gentlemen and gentlewomen. They identified with a much higher source of instruction, the Tao itself, and were not bound by the ties of obligation and servitude that Confucians held in such high regard. A.C. Graham describes them by saying, "The Taoist delight in the extraordinary is a protest against the imaginative poverty of Confucianism, a recovery of numinous wonder, a reversion to primitive and childlike vision."

The challenge and beauty of Taoism is that there is nothing to join, no vows to take, no ready-made lifestyle to take on. It is instead a path that constantly requires self cultivation, one's own difficult, yet rewarding journey to wholeness. It is through meditation, through qigong practice, through learning and applying the principles of *wu wei*, the wisdom of foolishness, the value of worthlessness and the uncarved block that we can recapture the sense of numinous wonder, of childlike vision that the ancient Taoists were famous for.

In a recent book entitled *The Healer Within*, author Roger Jahnke writes:

> When we learn to heal ourselves by activating our own internal medicine, we will be able to increase our productivity, our vitality, and our well being— three of the richest human assets—for free. The resulting revolution in self-reliance and personal empowerment will transform medicine, business, and even our communities.

Many of the practices and philosophies of Taoism are already entering the mainstream of Western society. Acupuncture, herbs, tai ji and now qigong are becoming more and more popular. National organizations are being formed with the purpose of educating society and supporting the growth of qigong and Taoist healing arts. More and more books, videos, tapes and conferences are being produced each year. Today Taoism is on the brink of becoming a major force in the spiritual life and well-being of Western society, much as Buddhism has been.

This work has been an attempt to introduce Western readers to a few of the attitudes, principles and practices of Taoism. It is by no means a comprehensive and complete work. There are many other sources available to the modern student who wishes to delve deeper into this subject.

Twenty-five hundred years ago Lao Tzu envisioned a society where each country had fewer people, machines were available to do work a hundred times faster than humans but the machines were not needed, where people had boats and carriages but didn't use them, where they had armor and weapons but did not display them, where food was plain yet good, clothes fine yet simple and homes were secure. People in this society were happy and though they lived within sight of each other they left each other in peace to grow old and die.

While this vision of society may seem simplistic in our day of modern technology and the global village, it is the spirit of this vision that is most important. A society that does not rely upon fast, dehumanizing technology; where people do not run from place to place but take their time to sink roots and get to know their environment intimately; where weapons exist but are not used; where food is nutritious and simple; where people can live safe and secure from foreign invasion or governmental suppression; where they can live in harmony with their neighbors whether they are in the next neighborhood or the next country; where they can honor each other's choice to live and worship in whatever way they see fit: that is a society we can all aspire to.

"When you learn the Way," says Hua-Ching Ni, "you come to know that the Way is in everybody and in everything. Applying the Way in your life makes your life fuller, more interesting, and more enjoyable."

As the Buddha lay dying he is supposed to have said, "Be a lamp unto yourself. Look to no outside help for your own salvation." So, too, do the Taoist sages of old hold up for us the untarnished mirror of our own self wisdom, reflecting the clarity of our own being. Lao Tzu says, "Knowing others is wisdom; knowing the self is enlightenment."

You have learned that one can know this elusive, seemingly invisible self through meditation, through studying the works of the ancients, through delving deeply into the murky depths of our being. You can also know the self by practicing qigong—the qigong of quiet reflection in the midst of activity; the qigong of balance, integrity and freeflowingness; the qigong of trusting in the beneficence and joyfulness of life; the qigong of trusting in your own innate and rarefied nature, the same nature as that of Tao itself; the qigong of learning to balance and harmonize with your often turbulent emotions; the qigong of sex and relationship; the qigong of allowing yourself to feel your own energy moving joyfully though the channels of your body; the qigong of learning to allow that energy flow, that joyfulness emerge and flow with others so that we can all join together in one great qigong dance.

We are all capable of becoming masters of our own destinies, directors of our own movies, creators of our own epics, lovers of our own lives. We can do this with grace, humility and thankfulness. Perhaps then we can become the person Lao Tzu describes who is able to see simplicity in the complicated and able to achieve greatness in little things. The line between confused human being and sage is, in reality, a thin and tenuous one. All it takes is being open to learning, growing, making mistakes, confronting our own fears and ambitions and a willingness to leap into the unknown.

Deng Ming Dao says:

> Sure we want to talk about how Taoism works in the West, how it's good for health and spirituality. One thing that people don't talk about very much is that there is something about it that is so precious, so special, something to really love and treasure. Once that opens for you there's no doubt in your mind about it. There's no end to the road you walk when you are on your path. That's something that I hope people will remember, that the path of Tao is a path that is very special and it is a living path that will provide for you forever once you get on it.

Being a Taoist means not being a blind follower of anyone or anything that is not natural, that is not aligned with the positive unfolding of the Tao itself. In the West there is no Taoist pope to lay down rules and regulations of what a Taoist should or should not be. Instead, Taoism is the process of learning how to connect with our own inner wisdom and guides so that we may better attune ourselves with the source of all wisdom and build our lives upon that.

The world today is in an unbalanced and inharmonious state in many ways. Perhaps each of us, through our own practices, through or own deep self cultivation, can help to affect this beloved world of ours so that someday everyone will be living in a qigong state of mind and body. Until then, we practice, study, experience and share. And in that sharing we grow and deepen and begin to understand and take Lao Tzu's advice when he said:

> Surrender yourself humbly; then you can be trusted to care for all things.
> Love the world as your own self; then you can truly care for all things.
> (Chapter 13)

Chapter Sources

Joseph Needham, *Science and Civilization In China*
A.C. Graham, *The Book of Lieh-tzu*
Hua-Ching Ni, *Mastering Chi*
Roger Jahnke, *The Healer Within*
Gia-Fu Feng and Jane English, *Tao Te Ching*
Deng Ming Dao, interview in *A Gathering of Cranes*

Recommended Reading

There are currently more and more books available about the Taoist arts. Here is a sampling of some of the best ones.

Beinfield, Harried and Korngold, Efrem. *Between Heaven and Earth: A Guide to Chinese Medicine.* New York: Ballantine Books, 1991.

Blofeld, John. *The Secret and the Sublime: Taoist Mysteries and Magic.* New York: E.P. Dutton & Co., 1973.

——*Taoism: The Road to Immortality.* Boston: Shambhala Publications Inc., 1978.

——*The Chinese Art of Tea.* Boston: Shambhala Publications Inc., 1985.

Chan, Luke. *101 Miracles of Natural Healing.* Cincinnati: Benefactor Press, 1996.

Chang, Jolan. *The Tao of Love and Sex.* New York: E.P.Dutton, 1977.

Chang, Stephen T. *The Tao of Sexology.* San Francisco: Tao Publishing, 1986.

Cheng, Man Ch'ing. *Cheng Tzu's Thirteen Treatises on T'ai Chi Ch'uan.* Translated by Benjamin Pang Jeng Lo and Martin Inn. Berkeley: North Atlan tic Books, 1985.

Chia, Mantak. *Awakening Healing Energy Through the Tao.* New York: Aurora Press, 1983.

——and Maneewan Chia. *Healing Love Through the Tao: Cultivating Fe-male Sexu ality.* Huntington, NY: Healing Tao Books, 1986.

——and Michael Winn, *Taoist Secrets of Love: Cultivating Male Sexuality.* New York: Aurora Press, 1984.

Chung, Tsai Chih. *Zhuangzi Speaks: The Music of Nature.* Translated by Brian Bruya. Princeton: Princeton University Press, 1992.

——*Tao Speaks: Lao-Tzu's Whispers of Wisdom.* Translated by Brian Bruya. New York: Doubleday, 1995.

Cleary, Thomas. *Immortal Sisters: Secrets of Taoist Women.* Boston: Shambhala Publications Inc., 1989.

——*Awakening to the Tao.* Boston: Shambhala Publications Inc., 1988.

——*The Inner Teachings of Taoism.* Boston: Shambhala Publications Inc., 1988.

——*Vitality, Energy, Spirit.* Boston: Shambhala Publications Inc., 1992.

——*The Book of Balance and Harmony.* San Francisco: North Point Press, 1989.

Cohen, Ken. *The Way of Qigong.* New York: Ballantine Books, 1997.

Cooper, J.C. *Chinese Alchemy.* Wellingborough: The Aquarian Press, 1984.

Feng, Gia-Fu and English, Jane. *Chuang Tsu: Inner Chapters.* Mt. Shasta, CA: Earth Heart, 1997.

——*Tao Te Ching.* New York: Alfred A. Knopf, 1972.

Fischer-Shreiber, Ingrid. *The Shambhala Dictionary of Taoism.* Boston:

Shambhala Publications Inc., 1996.

Flaws, Bob. *Imperial Secrets of Health and Longevity.* Boulder: Blue Poppy Press, 1994.

Graham, A.C. *The Book of Lieh-tzu.* New York: Columbia University Press, 1960.

Grigg, Ray. *The Tao of Zen.* Boston: Charles E. Tuttle Co., 1994.

Hoff, Benjamin. *The Tao of Pooh.* New York: Penguin Books, 1983.

Huang, Chungliang Al. *Tai Ji: The Beginner's Tai Ji Book.* Berkeley: Celestial Arts, 1989.

——*Embrace Tiger Return to Mountain.* Berkeley: Celestial Arts, 1997.

——& Lynch, Jerry. *Mentoring: The Tao of Giving and Receiving Wisdom.*New York: HarperSan Francisco, 1995.

Kaptchuk, Ted J., *The Web That Has No Weaver.* New York: Congdon & Weed Inc., 1983.

Kohn, Livia. *The Taoist Experience.* Albany: State University of New York Press, 1993.

——*Taoist Mystical Philosophy, The Scripture of Western Ascension.* Albany: State University of New York Press, 1991.

Jwing-Ming, Yang. *Tai Chi Chi Kung.* Jamaica Plain, MA: YMAA Publication Center, 1990.

——*The Root of Chinese Qigong.* Jamaica Plain, MA: YMAA Publication Center, 1997.

Jahnke, Roger. *The Healer Within.* New York: HarperSan Francisco, 1997.

Kaiguo, Chen & Shunchao Zheng. *Opening the Dragon Gate: The Making of a Modern Taoist Wizard.* Boston: Charles E. Tuttle Co., 1996.

Ke, Yun Lu. *The Essence of Qigong.* Eugene, OR: The Abode of the Eternal Tao, 1997.

Levy, Howard S. and Ishihara, Akira. *The Tao of Sex.* Lower Lake, CA: Integral Publishing, 1989.

Liu, Da. *T'ai Chi Ch'uan and Meditation.* New York: Schocken Books, 1986.

Mair, Victor H. *Wandering On the Way: Early Taoist Tales and Parables of Chuang Tzu.* New York: Bantam Books, 1994.

MacRitchie, James. *The Chi Kung Way.* San Francisco: Harper Collins, 1997.

Ming-Dao, Deng. *Scholar Warrior.* New York: HarperSan Francisco, 1990.

——*Chronicles of Tao.* New York: HarperSan Francisco, 1993.

——*Everyday Tao.* New York: HarperSan Francisco, 1996.

——*365 Tao.* New York: HarperSan Francisco, 1992.

Ni, Hua-Ching. *The Book of Changes and the Unchanging Truth.* Santa Monica, CA: Seven Star Communications, 1990.

——*Mastering Chi.* Santa Monica, CA: Seven Star Communications, 1994.

——*Mysticism, Empowering the Spirit Within.* Santa Monica, CA: Seven Star Communications, 1992.

——*Internal Alchemy, The Natural Way to Immortality.* Santa Monica, CA: Seven Star Communications, 1992.

——*Tao: The Subtle Universal Law and the Integral Way of Life.* Santa Monica, CA: Seven Star Communications, 1995.

Ni, Maoshing. *The Yellow Emperor's Classic of Medicine.* Boston: Shambhala Publications Inc., 1995.

Porter, Bill. *Road to Heaven: Encounters with Chinese Hermits*. San Francisco: Mercury House, 1993.

Reid, Daniel. *The Complete Book of Chinese Health and Healing*. Boston: Shambhala Publications Inc., 1994.

——*The Tao of Health, Sex, and Longevity*. New York and London: Simon & Schuster, 1989.

Robinet, Isabelle. *Taoist Meditation, The Mao-Shan Tradition of Great Purity*. Albany: State University of New York Press, 1993.

Schipper, Kristofer. *The Taoist Body*. Berkeley: University of California Press, 1993.

Smullyan,Raymond. *The Tao Is Silent*. New York: HarperSan Francisco, 1977.

Towler, Solala. *A Gathering of Cranes, Bringing the Tao to the West*. Eugene, OR: The Abode of the Eternal Tao, 1996.

Unschuld, Paul U. *Medicine in China: A History of Ideas*. Berkeley: University of California Press, 1985.

Van Gulik, R.H. *Sexual Life in Ancient China*. Leiden: E.J. Brill, 1974.

Waltham, Clae. *Chuang Tzu: Genius of the Absurd*. New York: Ave Books, 1971.

Ware, James R. *Alchemy, Medicine & Religion in the China of A.D. 320: The Nei P'ien Ko Hung*. Boston: Dover Publications, 1996.

Watts, Alan. *Tao: The Watercourse Way*. New York: Pantheon Books, 1975.

——*The Tao of Philosophy*. Boston: Charles E. Tuttle Co., Inc., 1995.

Wile, Douglas. *Art of the Bedchamber: The Chinese Sexual Yoga Classics Including Women's Solo Meditation Texts*. Albany: State University of New York Press, 1992.

Wong, Eva. *Lieh-Tzu, A Taoist Guide to Practical Living*. Boston: Shambhala Publications Inc., 1995.

——*Cultivating Stillness*. Boston: Shambhala Publications Inc., 1992.

——*Feng-Shui: The Harmonious Wisdom of Harmonious Living for Modern Times*. Boston: Shambhala Publications Inc., 1996.

——Teachings of Tao. Boston: Shambhala Publications Inc., 1997.

——*The Shambhala Guide to Taoism*. Boston: Shambhala Publications Inc., 1997.

Yan, Xin. *Secrets and Benefits of Internal Qigong Cultivation*. Malvern, PA: Amber Leaf Press, 1997.

Other Resources

The Abode of the Eternal Tao
1991 Garfield St., Eugene, OR 97405
Tel/Fax: 541-345-8854
web site: http://www.abodetao.com
Publishes magazine *The Empty Vessel: A Journal of Contemporary Taoism and books on contemporary Taoism.*
Also offers classes on several styles of qigong and Taoist meditation and sponsors a yearly Exploring the Terrain of Taoist China tour.

Living Tao Foundation
Lan Ting Institute
PO Box 846, Urbana, IL 61803
Tel/Fax: 217-337-6113
Living Tao Foundation is a nonprofit global membership network founded in 1976 by Chungliang Al Huang. It offers national and international seminars and training programs in Taoist principles applicable to successful modern living. The focus is on Taoist classics, tai ji movement and its related disciplines as mirror reflections of our lifelong learning process.

Universal Society of the Integral Way
PO Box 28993, Atlanta, GA 30358
770-392-9605
website: http://www.usiw.org/
The USIW is a nonprofit, nondenominational, nonpartisan and spiritually focused organization of individuals dedicated to supporting the self-development of all people. Its mission is to assist people throughout the world in achieving physical, mental and spiritual health by nurturing individual self-respect and by offering time-tested methods of individual self-improvement based on the principles of the *I Ching* and of Lao Tzu's *Tao Te Ching*. Further elucidation of these ancient teachings by Hua-Ching Ni provides the foundation of the USIW's spiritual purpose and direction.

Chi Kung/Qigong Association of America
571 Selby Ave., St. Paul, MN 55102
Tel: 888-218-7788 Fax: 612-291-7779
A national organization dedicated to education and support of qigong in the United States. Organizes yearly national conference and regional seminars. National network for referral to accredited teachers and healers.

Index

A

B

C

D

Other publications by
The Abode of the Eternal Tao

A Gathering of Cranes, Bringing the Tao to the West
by Solala Towler

In this volume of interviews with nine well-known authors and teachers who have brought Taoism from China to the West, we learn the wisdom and experiences of Taoism including: meditation, qigong, tai ji, Chinese medicine and receive guidance on how to live a healthy and long-lasting life—mentally, spiritually and physically.

Softcover, 150 pages, $12.95

The Essence of Qigong : A Handbook of Theory and Practice
(First time in English!)
by Ke Lun Yu

This book by the well-known Chinese author introduces the basic theories and guidelines to qigong in order to provide a solid foundation for the modern practitioner, no matter which particular style he or she chooses to learn. Guidance is provided on psychic experiences as well as qigong healing. Also included are sections on the relationship of qigong to modern science as well as other paths, including Buddhism, Taoism and Christianity. In this way this book appeals to both the beginning as well as the longtime student of qigong.

Softcover, 150 pages, $14.95

The Empty Vessel, A Journal of Contemporary Taoism

A quarterly publication dedicated to the exploration and dissemination of nonreligious Taoist philosophy and practice. Learn practical applications of Taoist thought, tai ji, internal arts, Chinese medicine and qigong. Enjoy articles, interviews and feature stories that show how contemporary practitioners have incorporated a balance of body, mind and spirit into their lives.

Includes art, poetry, essays and reviews of the latest books, tapes and videos. *The Empty Vessel* is the only journal of its kind, covering all aspects of Taoist philosophy and practice in a thought-provoking and timely manner.

Subscriptions are $18 per year. Sample issue $6.50 postpaid.

The Abode of the Eternal Tao
1991 Garfield St.
Eugene, OR 97405
Toll-free order line: 1-800-574-5118